ERIN'S DIARY

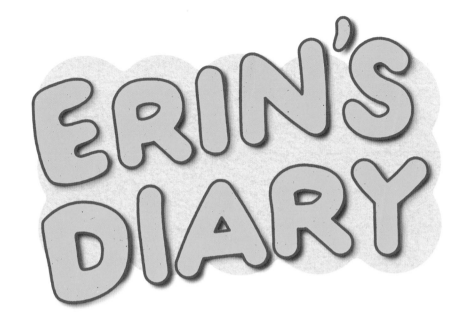

ERIN'S DIARY

An Official

DERRY GIRLS

BOOK

LISA MCGEE

TRAPEZE

First published in Great Britain in 2020 by Trapeze
an imprint of The Orion Publishing Group Ltd
Carmelite House, 50 Victoria Embankment
London EC4Y 0DZ

An Hachette UK Company

1 3 5 7 9 10 8 6 4 2

A CIP catalogue record for this book is
available from the British Library.

ISBN (Hardback) 9781841884394
ISBN (eBook) 9781841884424

Designed by us-now.com
Printed in Germany

FSC
www.fsc.org

www.orionbooks.co.uk

For John Hume.
Thank you for giving Derry Girls like me a better future.

DEDICATION

For the people of Derry.

Who laughed at my ambition and called me a mouth*.

Well, who's laughing now!

*Check my glossary

ACKNOWLEDGEMENTS

1ST DRAFT

(So this is the bit where the author usually thanks the people in their life who helped them while writing the book, but I don't really think any of my family or friends deserve a mention to be honest, so I'm just gonna skip it.)

INTELLECTUAL QUOTE

I think I should open with a quote from Seamus Heaney, as he's my second

favourite poet. I could quote my first favourite poet but – well, is it a bit weird

to quote myself in my own book? No, I'm not doing that. I'm just too modest.

Between my finger and my thumb
The squat pen rests.
I'll dig with it.
– Seamus Heaney

Yeah that's good. Very profound. Yeah I'm definitely going to go with

that. Well either that or the chorus of 'Hero' by Mariah Carey.

Hmmm. Can't decide.

I CAN DO IT!

NOTES

Possible titles for inevitable publication:

1. The Life and Times of Erin Quinn by Erin Quinn

2. The Erin Quinn Story by Erin Quinn

3. The Trouble with The Troubles by Erin Quinn-Donnelly (might have married David Donnelly by the time this hits the shelves)

4. Derry Product by Erin Quinn (pun on words — will people get it???)

5. The Life and Legacy of Erin Quinn by Erin Quinn (do you have to be dead to have a legacy?? Need to check this)

6. The Gospel According to Erin Quinn (might be blasphemy? Don't want to piss off Jesus)

7. Heart of Erin by Erin Quinn (clever double meaning because Erin means Ireland — but is it maybe too clever??)

GLOSSARY

I've endeavoured to keep these memoirs as authentic as possible. Therefore, I occasionally use colloquialisms. I've marked these up with asterisks. The glossary below should help non-Derry natives navigate the pages that follow.

Aye: Yes.

Bars: Gossip/scandal. E.g. "Have you any bars for me?" Origin: some say when Derry's female shirt factory workers had exciting or scandalous news they would tap the metal bar above their sewing machine to alert their co-workers. This may well be completely made up.

Blocked: Drunk.

Boke: Vomit.

Bokeorama: A lot of vomit.

Brit: A member of the British Armed Forces.

Broke: Embarrassed.

Broke to the bone: Hugely embarrassed.

Buncrana: A popular holiday destination.

Buzzing: Very happy. E.g. to be buzzing out of one's tree.

Cack attack: A state of extreme nervousness. E.g. "I'm having a complete cack attack."

Can't hold their water: Someone who is very indiscreet.

Catch yourself on: Don't be so ridiculous.

Chicken Ball Special: Authentic Chinese delicacy only available in Derry.

Class: Brilliant.

Clattered: To be covered in something. E.g. "I was clattered in paint."

Craic: "Fun" or "news". E.g. "The craic was great" or "Have you any craic for me?" Important: use with caution, particularly when travelling. My cousin Nuala once asked someone if they "had any craic" in a Boston pub and wound up spending the night in jail.

Cracker: Beyond brilliant.

Critter: Someone who evokes sympathy. E.g. "You poor critter."

Dicko: A general insult.

Doherty's special mince: The only mince permissible by law in Derry.

Dose: An unbearable human being.

Eejit: An idiot.

Fenian: Offensive term for a Catholic unless a Catholic is using it to describe Catholics in which case it's sort of fine.

Football Special: The nicest non-alcoholic beverage in the world.

Free State: The Republic of Ireland.

Gone: Please. E.g. "Gone give me that."

Head melter: Someone who causes you mental distress.

Hi: A sound placed at the end of almost every sentence for no particular reason. E.g. "No problem hi."

Hole: Backside.

IRA: Irish Republican Army.

Jaffa: Offensive term for a Protestant.

John Hume: The MP for Foyle (Derry City). General good egg.

John Hume's office: A place people ring/visit in the hope of solving a wide variety of problems.

Lurred: Absolutely delighted. Origins of this one uncertain. Some people attribute it to the Catholic pilgrimage site of Lourdes in southwestern France, i.e. a feeling of religious ecstasy. Though I can find no evidence to back up this claim.

Mind: Remember. E.g. "Do you mind the time I fell down the stairs?"

Mouth: Someone prone to exaggeration.

Mucker: Friend.

No bother at all: This is absolutely no trouble in the slightest and I'd be thrilled to help. Not to be confused with **A bit of bother:** This is a huge amount of trouble and I resent being asked to help.

Not a baldies: No idea.

Orange Order: Conservative Unionist organisation who enjoy marching.

Provo: A member of the Provisional IRA.

Punt: Currency of the Free State, aka the Republic of Ireland.

Raging: Annoyed/angry.

Ride (n): A very attractive person.

Ride (v): To have sex.

Ripping: Extremely annoyed/angry. FYI – a **"Riptor scale"** may be used to indicate just how ripping a person is. At the lower end there's **Angela Ripping,** e.g. "I was a bit Angela Ripping, to be honest," and at the upper end we have **Jack the Ripping,** e.g. "I am absolutely Jack the Ripping." If you're particularly upset about something you might even be **"off the Riptor scale"**.

RUC: The Royal Ulster Constabulary (the cops).

Ruined: Spoilt rotten.

Saunter: To stroll about in a playful manner. Also, an insult. E.g. "Saunter on – please be on your way."

Shite the tights: Someone of a nervous disposition.

Slabber: A show-off.

So it is/So I am: A phrase used for emphasis. E.g. "I'm delighted so I am."

Spoof: Fake or counterfeit goods. E.g. "That's a spoof fiver."

Spoofing: Being loose with the truth.

Stall the ball: Stop what you're doing immediately.

Start: To provoke. E.g. "Don't start me."

Steaming: Drunk.

Swipe/Swiped: Steal/stole.

Tayto sandwich: A cheese and onion crisp sandwich, a local delicacy.

'The Late Late Toy Show': Cultural event of the year.

UDA: Ulster Defence Association.

Wain: A child or young person.

Watch yourself now: Take care.

Whack: An unspecified amount.

Wile: Very or terrible. E.g. "I'm wile hungry"/"She's having a wile time of it."

Wise up: "Don't be so stupid and/or immature."

Yes: Hello. E.g. "Yes, what about you?" = "Hello, how are you?"

INTRODUCTION

~~Hello Friend,~~

~~Where to begin? At the start is as good a place as any, I imagine.~~

That's shit. Maybe start with a joke???

B.F.F.

Erin Quinn

INTRODUCTION

Hello there,

My name is Erin Quinn. But then you already know that. You bought this book and my name is on the cover...Ha ha!

Wise up Erin!

Erin Quinn

Erin Quinn Donnelly

Erin Quinn

DERRY

Erin

Erin Quinn Donnelly

INTRODUCTION

Dear Reader,

It is a pleasure to introduce you to this, my memoirs.

Now. Where to begin?

People often ask if I knew I'd grow up to be a world-renowned writer.

In many ways I suppose I did. My earliest memory is being just nine months old. I grabbed hold of a purple crayon with my chubby little hands and started scrawling out a story. Obviously, it didn't make sense. I couldn't actually spell or anything — I was nine months old — I mean, that would have made me some sort of freak. No, it was just a load of random squiggles, really. I also did it on the living room wall, which wasn't great as my da had only just papered it. I think he cried, actually. Anyway, my point is the instinct was there. Writing wasn't a choice. It was a calling.

Though my journey has not been without its difficulties. Growing up amid a bloody sectarian conflict has been challenging: the bullets, the bombs, the guns. Indeed, I am no stranger to oppression. After all, our streets are patrolled by monsters who continually abuse their authority. They are cold and militant. Always watching us. Following us. They search our bags and pat down our bodies, aggressively barking their questions: "Where are you going? What are you hiding?" Then come the accusations: "You're lying!" And of course the threats: "I will not ask you again." These people don't care about our rights. They don't care about our dignity. God, but Mammies really are the worst.

I could play the victim, but these traumatic experiences have made me the artist I am today, a prolific writer with an impressive (some might even say intimidating) body of work.

(Note to self: double-check the meaning of prolific.)

My back catalogue of plays and short stories speaks for itself and my academic essays have been incredibly well received (B– in my English mock, thank you very much!). But I think perhaps it's my poetry that I will be most remembered for.

21 College Gardens,
Belfast BT9 6WV

6th December

Dear Miss Quinn,

Thank you very much for your prompt reply to the letter we sent you rejecting your poem 'Crossfire Child'.

I am extremely sorry to hear that you feel our views are "pedestrian" and that we lack "vision and soul". I can only reiterate that while we are of course always keen to encourage new writers, pieces running to several pages of verse – twenty-three, if I recall correctly – are by necessity somewhat difficult to publish.

I appreciate your grandfather Joe's high estimation of your literary output, and can only apologise profusely (again) that this piece of work is not for us.

The most important thing, of course, is to keep writing, and I wish you well with that.

All the best,

Trevor McHenry
Editor, 'New Ulster Poets Now!'

Verse 1: 'Crossfire Child' by Erin Quinn

I see it all as though it were a dream

My life, the carnage and the trouble

But what, if anything, can it mean?

If the play's played out in between this rubble

If below the city walls we all must huddle

If our loved ones are not here to cuddle

Why must we live in this bubble?

TO-DO LIST

1. Get a professional headshot taken for back cover.

2. Ask Mammy for money to pay for professional headshot for back cover.

1st JANUARY

My name is Erin Quinn. I'm sixteen years old and I come from a place called Derry — or Londonderry, depending on your persuasion — a troubled little corner in the northwest of Ireland. It's fair to say I have a somewhat complicated relationship with my home town. You see, the thing about living in Derry is, there's nowhere to hide. Everybody knows everybody, knows everything about everybody, and sometimes all I really want is to be simply left alone.

(Wow! Just read that back to myself. V. powerful.)

My friend Clare gave me this notebook for Christmas, and I think I'm going to use it as a diary. I mean, all the great writers kept diaries and it seems a bit shameful that I've never actually managed it before.

But this year is different. It has to be, because these are extraordinary times in Derry — historically, politically and culturally — and I suspect that it may soon become clear that I'm...well, the voice of a generation. It feels only fair on those coming behind me that I record every thought and feeling I have in rigorous detail.

2ND JANUARY

Ate a Mars bar. It was nice.

3RD JANUARY

Clare is thinking of getting a fringe, which I said would be a **MASSIVE MISTAKE.** Now she's huffing.

4TH JANUARY

Had this really, really weird dream last night. There was this storm and I got carried off to this magical kingdom where all the animals could talk, even the trees could talk, and I started hanging around with this, like, mannequin fella, and this robot and this tiger. The three of them were really useless and expected me to sort out all their stupid problems and I was a bit, like, "I've had enough of this craic*, I just want to go home." Then I woke up.

I've been thinking — what if this world that we call reality is actually the dream world and our dreams are actually the reality?

That's so deep I just gave myself a bit of a headache.

I think my dream would be a really good idea for a movie! I'm gonna start working on the script right now. Or maybe I'll do it after 'Home and Away'.

5TH JANUARY

So Michelle said my dream is basically just the plot of 'The Wizard of Oz'. Which makes a lot of sense. I've seen it, like, a hundred times. I even have a dog called Toto. Glad I didn't waste any time writing that script now.

6TH JANUARY

6pm

I was thinking I might need to include more "historical context" in these diaries because once they're published they're gonna be sold all around the world, and people in Brazil or Malaysia or Hawaii aren't gonna have a baldies* about the political situation here. I find it hard enough to follow myself, to be honest. Gonna go downstairs now and watch the news to bring myself up to speed.

7pm

Ian Paisley is absolutely ripping* with the IRA. Derry might be getting a Pizza Hut.

11TH JANUARY

Clare got the fringe and to be fair it does really suit her.

12TH JANUARY

Maybe I should get a fringe.

15TH JANUARY

Why the **HELL** did I get this fringe?? I hate it. I look like a spud.

16TH JANUARY

MAJOR NEWS – Michelle just rang. She went to the under-18 disco at the Bogside community centre last night. Of course my ma didn't let me go...again. I'm actually considering exploring my legal options now. What's she's doing is essentially forced confinement. It's going to have a detrimental effect on my growth and development. I mean, I haven't even kissed a boy yet (I practise on my pillow sometimes but I don't think that's the same) and Michelle has already **LOST HER VIRGINITY!** That's right. She got off with some fella called Marty who she claims is the spit of Jason Priestley. I'm not so sure – I think if there was a Jason Priestley lookalike knocking about Derry, I might know about it. Anyway, she went back to his place (his ma and da were out at the St Columb's Hall dinner dance) and they **DID THE DEED.** She couldn't really go into details over the phone but she's gonna call round in a bit and fill me in. I cannot believe it!!!

17TH JANUARY

So Michelle hasn't lost her virginity. From what she told me last night I'd say she's lost half of it. Two-thirds at most. She's **SUCH** a mouth*.

Book Launch Invite List

Just figuring out some plans for my book launch when these memoirs are published. What will I wear?

A simple and chic black mini dress, neck scarf, minimal jewellery and an enigmatic expression. Who is invited?

1. David Donnelly - Date.
   We will definitely be going out by then.
2. Mammy
3. Daddy
4. Granda
5. Aunt Sarah
6. Cousin Orla (Mammy will make me)
7. Baby Anna
8. Clare Devlin (BF)
9. Michelle Mallon (Joint BF)
10. Jenny Joyce (For making her jealous reasons)
11. Sister Michael
    (For proving she was wrong about me reasons)

TO-DO LIST – UPDATE

1. Mammy is refusing to give me the money to get my headshots done even though it's only a loan and I will pay her back as soon as I have my advance from the book deal. She is just **SO IMPOSSIBLE!**

2. Jim across the road has a professional camera. Orla is going to ask him if we can borrow it and she can take some shots of me. How hard can it be?

3. Must grow this fringe out ASAP.

30TH JANUARY

So I caught Orla snooping around my room again. I'm gonna have to find a better hiding place for this diary because I really can't have her reading it...it's pretty explosive stuff.

28TH AUGUST

Okay, hid this thing a bit too well. Been looking for it for the last seven months.

Important:
Check Orla has camera turned right
way round at next photoshoot session.

29th AUGUST

Here is the list of resolutions Clare and I made this week for the new school year:

1. Be individuals. Obviously my ma didn't purchase a Levi's red tab denim jacket **AS I REQUESTED!** Instead she got me a spoof* one from the market. Its label says 'Pevi' — mortifying. I'll just have to make sure nobody gets close enough to read it. This is like the fake Kickers fiasco all over again.

2. We will get boyfriends.

3. We couldn't actually think of any more.

SPONSORSHIP FORM

Name: Clare Devlin

is asking you to sponsor her 24-hour fast.

Kamal is only ten years old, and yet he has to walk
twenty-five miles every day just to fetch his family drinking water.
Your support will help Irish Aid for Africa build a well in Kamal's village.

NAME	AMOUNT
Geraldine Devlin	£2
Sean Devlin	£2
Nanny Clare	£2
Aunt Marie	£2
Uncle Tommy	50p (Apparently he's not made of money)
Pirate Pauline	Promised £2 as soon as her dole comes through
Erin Quinn	£2
Miss Mooney	£2

31St AUGUSt

First day of school tomorrow and I'm actually really looking forward to it. I just know I'm going to achieve a lot this year, personally, academically, artistically. Yes, it feels very much like this is my time.

1St SePtemBeR

Jesus Christ! Where do I start? Okay, it wasn't all bad, I suppose.

Positives:

1. David Donnelly definitely fancies me. He asked me out on a date outside Dennis's Wee Shop this morning. (I'm very, very concerned about Dennis's blood pressure btw – but that's another story.) God, David is just such a ride*, I can't cope.

2. Clare raised £33 for Africa.

Negatives:

1. Jenny Joyce has been made prefect!

2. Orla's been reading my diary.

3. Clare broke her fast and had to give the £33 back.

4. We've been accused of murdering a nun.

As if I didn't have enough to do with exams coming up, now I'm at the centre of a miscarriage of justice and have to clear my name. Apart from anything else this could really impact my book sales. At the risk of sounding like Clare, it's all Michelle's fault. We wouldn't even have been in detention if she hadn't threatened wee Tina whose sister Mandy is a bona fide psychopath and will definitely seek vengeance. Honestly, Michelle is such a liability. Anyway, I'm innocent. I played no part in Sister Declan's death. The truth will out.

Oh God...

Something just occurred to me...I mean, I 100 per cent stand by the fact that I had nothing to do with Sister Declan's sudden death. No one could have predicted her keeling over like that. But come to think of it, she did expire just as she was really getting her nose in amongst the writing in this book. Maybe she'd read some of my poetry. Is it possible that it is just, like, so profound and affecting that it killed her???

David Donnelly
xoxox
Erin Quinn
21120
3232
555
1010
111
22%
↑
total balls

(Note to self: maybe tear out the previous paragraph? Could be incriminating?)

And poor David Donnelly! I mean, he finally plucked up the courage to ask me out and now he must think I stood him up. That's the real tragedy in all this.

Oh, I forgot to mention, Michelle brought her cousin to school today. English fella. Not much to look at. John, I think she said his name was. Seems like a bit of a drip.

Correction: Apparently his name is James.

Book Launch Invite List <u>updated</u>

1. David Donnelly - Date.
   We will definitely be going out by then.

2. ~~Mammy~~ Now banned as she
   clearly doesn't believe in me.

3. Daddy

4. Granda

5. Aunt Sarah

6. ~~Cousin Orla (Mammy will make me)~~ Banned
   - no respect for
     personal boundaries.

7. Baby Anna

8. Clare Devlin (BF)

9. ~~Michelle Mallon (Joint BF)~~ Banned. Is liability.

10. Jenny Joyce (For making her jealous reasons)

11. Sister Michael
    (For proving she was wrong about me reasons)

THE HOLY SACRIFICE OF THE MASS WILL BE OFFERED FOR THE REPOSE OF THE SOUL OF:

Sister Declan

....

BY FATHER:

Conway

....

WITH THE SYMPATHY OF:

The Quinn Family

....

15th September

I have **HAD IT** with Jenny Joyce! I've tried to be reasonable but there's no talking to her. She's been on a total power trip ever since she's become prefect. Assembly performances are supposed to rotate. But she has the whole thing sewn up. And I'm sorry but that singing teacher of hers is taking the piss – she's getting worse, if anything. I've written this absolutely brilliant play – it's set in Derry and a sort of modern reimagining of 'Romeo and Juliet' only…and this is the genius bit… Romeo is a Catholic and Juliet is a Protestant. It's just **SO** original and ground-breaking. But Jenny is refusing to let us perform it. I mean, sure it's a bold interpretation, risky in some places, downright shocking in others. But that's what great art is supposed to do: shock us, shake things up a bit. Not that Jenny cares about art. All she cares about is being in charge. She's a **CONTROL FREAK!** I tried to complain to Sister Michael, who just looked me up and down and said, "I'm finding it very difficult to make myself care." The whole system is corrupt. Once this book is published, the entire world will see Our Lady Immaculate College for the rotten institution that it really is. **THEY'LL BE SORRY.**

18th September

So, Sister Michael says I can perform my play at assembly as long as I let Jenny be in it. **HAPPY DAYS!**

Julie and Ryan
By Erin Josephine Quinn

. . . .

Eleventh Night of July. A bonfire rages on stage (<u>may need to flag this up to Sister Michael – could be a Health and Safety concern?</u>)

<u>Julie:</u> Come with me, my love.

<u>Ryan:</u> To the bonfire? Are you wise? They'd throw me on it!

<u>Julie:</u> Not the bonfire. I know I could never reconcile you to that pagan display of crushing imperialist occupation. No, let's run away.

<u>Ryan:</u> We can't, Julie. I'm but a poor Fenian* and you're a rich Prod. The odds are stacked against us.

<u>Julie:</u> But I love you.

<u>Ryan:</u> I love you too

They kiss passionately.

<u>Ryan:</u> I can't breathe.

<u>Julie:</u> Yes. I feel the same when I'm with you, Ryan.

<u>Ryan:</u> No, I mean the smoke. That bloody bonfire. I have asthma, you know. This is desperate.

<u>Julie:</u> This place is suffocating us, Ryan! Don't you see?!

<u>Ryan:</u> I don't even have my inhaler with me.

<u>Julie:</u> Let's just go. Let's leave everything and everyone behind. Let's go somewhere we can be free. Somewhere we don't have to be Protestant or Catholic, or British or Irish, or Unionist or Nationalist. Somewhere we can simply be Julie and Ryan – two young people in love.

<u>Ryan:</u> What about Buncrana*?

<u>Julie:</u> (Smiles) Buncrana*, here we come!

They exit stage left, hand in hand.

. . . .

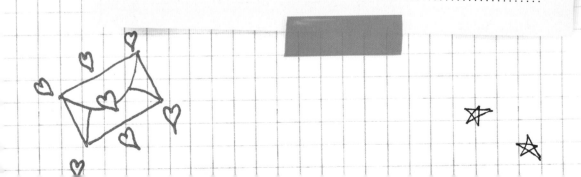

1st October

MAJOR DRAMA! So my aunt Sarah and cousin Orla live next door.
Well, it's probably more accurate to say they sleep next door. They
spend every other waking moment in our house. Last night they heard
a scratching sound coming from the skirting boards. Despite Orla's
insistence that it was a Borrower (several of her blazer buttons have
recently disappeared), it became clear that it was a mouse...boke* .

Daddy suggested we ask Maureen Malarkey if we could borrow her cat
Tigger but Maureen and Granda had a massive fallout at the bingo last
week so that was a no go. Instead, Granda asked Jim across the road to
bring over his airgun and they tried to shoot it. They missed and hit the
fuse box so now there's no electricity. Aunt Sarah's afraid to go back in
while the mouse is still there but she's also a bit concerned it could claim
squatters' rights. Daddy tried to reassure her that this is very unlikely
because...well...it's a rodent. But she's gonna ring John Hume's office*
anyway just to double-check.

Then Mammy decided to take matters into her own hands. She went
next door and drenched the place with holy water. I'm not sure how long
a mouse exorcism takes but Aunt Sarah and Orla are staying tonight
just to be safe. Aunt Sarah's gonna sleep in my room, which means me
and Orla will have to top and tail on Jim's airbed in the living room.
I HATE my life.

Dear Borrowers,

I know we all have to live under the same roof but this is getting ridiculous – I leave something down for **ONE SECOND** and you're off with it. I'm not that bothered about the blazer buttons or the Lego, but I need my hotdog pencil sharpener and tiny terrapin collection back immediately.

You have until 6pm tomorrow evening.

All the best

Orla McCool

2ND OCTOBER

So, despite me constructing a barrier with cushions, Orla kept encroaching on my side of the airbed and I didn't get a wink. Then I go up to my room to get ready only to discover Aunt Sarah has left an impression of her entire body on my bedsheet – why does she have to wear so much fake tan?! Honestly, it's like the Shroud of Turin.

I complained about it to Mammy and she pretended to sympathise, but I know she's secretly buzzing* because it means she can do a boil wash.

5TH OCTOBER

Learned the rap bit from 'Rhythm is a Dancer'.

Tel: 0504 649 6412
Fax: 0504 649 6414

Our Lady Immaculate College

Dear Parents and Guardians,

It is my reluctant duty to inform you that Mr Macaulay in his infinite wisdom has decided that this year's destination for the Euro Trotters trip will be Paris. The overall price for the five-day stay is £350. There was a discussion about the school potentially subsidising part of the cost, but unfortunately that wasn't possible in the end because I didn't want to do it. If you have any further questions please direct them to Mr Macaulay as I have decided to wash my hands of the whole affair.

Regards,

Sr. Michael

Sr Michael

Principal

Directors: Father John O'Brien, Cllr. Michael Kennedy, Mr. Conor McCarthy, Mrs. Aoife Moore. Registered in Belfast. Company No. 8769521

21st OCTOBER

4pm

Paris! I cannot believe I'm going to Paris! The Arc de Triomphe, the Champs-Élysées, the Louvre. The home of Beckett and the Moulin Rouge and "Allo 'Allo!' I'm gonna sit in quaint little cafes sipping coffee, eating croissants and writing poetry. I feel like finally I'll belong. I've only ever seen Paris in the movies. God, but I just love French movies. 'Three Colours Blue' is probably my favourite film of all time.

(Note to self: if you are going to include the 'Three Colours Blue' thing in these memoirs, **MAKE SURE** you actually watch it before they get published — you might get asked about it in press interviews and that could be embarrassing.)

We were all worried Paris was a bit expensive but Jenny Joyce wasn't being a total dose* for once and explained about the whole Trust Fund thing. If, like us, you'd never heard of a Trust Fund before, it's basically this account your parents set up for you when you're born and then they put loads and loads of money in it. I guess my ma and da haven't mentioned it before because they don't want me dipping into it constantly for stupid things...but a trip to Paris is of **HUGE** educational value so I'm sure they won't have any issue with me making a withdrawal.

There is just one problem. Charlene Kavanagh, who is the most popular and best-looking girl at school, is also going on the trip and asked me to hang out with her when we're there. Obviously, this is her way of asking me to join her gang permanently, which isn't surprising really. Despite the fact that she's never actually spoken to me before, I've always thought we had a connection. If I decide to join Charlene's gang, it means cutting ties with my current one. Orla, Clare, Michelle and James aren't really Charlene's type of people...they're a bit immature and, well, I don't want to say dull but...(can't actually think of a less insulting word than dull so will change this when I do my first round of edits).

This is all quite tricky. Charlene and I are a much better fit friendship wise but I've just known the girls for so long. I mean, Orla's family. They'll be really hurt. So even though in many ways I have outgrown them, I can't just dump them. Perhaps I'm simply too loyal for my own good.

4.15pm

I think I am gonna dump them, actually. They're holding me back.

Right, better go downstairs and ask Mammy how to access this Trust Fund. May also have to withdraw some money for a new wardrobe. My current threads are very un-Parisian.

Trust Fund stuff

Me and the gang put together this list of stuff we want to buy with our Trust Fund money. We thought we'd bunch together and share some items rather than buying five of everything – which might be a bit extravagant.

1. New pencil case x5
2. Curling tongs
3. Light-up mirror x2
4. Disposable camera
5. A Talkboy
6. A ream of paper
7. Metallic gel pens x5
8. A couple of those rings that open and have lip balm inside
9. A three-litre bottle of vodka
10. Red Tab Levi's (non spoof*) x4
11. A Soda Stream
12. Bottle of CK1 x5
13. A skateboard
14. A step aerobics step
15. A Tamagotchi
16. A Lava Lamp

17. 'Murder, She Wrote' VHS
18. Yankee Candle x5
19. A briefcase
20. A wee something for Kamal
21. A Slush Puppy machine
22. A portable TV
23. A boob job
24. A trip to Planet Hollywood x5
25. A swimming pool
26. A revolving wardrobe like Cher in 'Clueless'
27. A trip to Disneyland x5
28. A cruise x5
29. A car x5
30. A house in Donegal (five bedrooms)

5pm

I'm gonna **KILL** Jenny Joyce! There is no Trust Fund. There's no funds at all, according to my ma. We're poor. Poor! I can't believe it! I mean, I always knew we weren't like...the Banks family from 'The Fresh Prince of Bel Air' or anything...like, we don't have a butler...but poor! This is just really shit. I mean, I know I won't always be poor...there's definitely going to be a bidding war for this book and then there will obviously be the movie franchise, etc. but right now it's no money, no Paris, no Charlene Kavanagh. I'm supposed to be going to the chip shop now but I just don't have any appetite. I couldn't manage a bite. I'm too depressed.

I mean, maybe a small battered hotdog but even that would be a struggle.

A portion of onion rings at a push.

Possibly a handful of chips. But I mean a handful.

Fionnula's
FISH & CHIPS

1 portion red fish
1 portion white fish
~~2 x bags of chips~~
~~3 x bags of chips~~
~~4 x bags of chips~~
12 chicken nuggets
Small battered hotdog x 2 (onions and sauce)
~~5 bags of chips~~
1 PLAIN chicken burger
Steak and kidney pie
~~6 bags of chips~~
curry dip
garlic mayo dip
gravy dip
taco dip
7 bags of chips

11.30pm

Sorry it's so late. Uncle Colm showed up. I don't know what he was going on about. To be honest, I stopped listening. I think maybe someone tried to kidnap him, but he was so boring they brought him back?? I'll ask my ma the right way of it tomorrow. He's still here so I'm hiding. Anyway, some good news. Everyone else is poor too. Yay! Apparently Derry is quite a poor place, which is great. I mean, obviously it's not great but at least I'm not on my own. Also we're back in play with Paris. Clare had this genius idea – we all get part-time jobs and pay for it ourselves. Isn't that brilliant? I think relying on your parents for money is a bit pathetic, actually. I'd much rather make my own way in the world. You might have a Trust Fund, Jenny, but you don't have the moral high ground!!

So, there was quite a few of these job things advertised on the chip shop noticeboard and...well, to cut a long story short, Michelle swiped* it...the entire noticeboard. There was some debate as to whether this was the wisest move but it's done now and, to be fair to Michelle, we do have first dibs on some potentially lucrative positions – dog walker, babysitter and gardener to name but a few. I'm sure they all pay really well! Paris, here we come!

My only concern is that Fionnula (purveyor of chips/owner of noticeboard/psychopath) finds out about this. She can never know.

23RD OCTOBER

Fionnula knows!

Clare told her mother all about it. I should have guessed she would. Clare can't hold her water*. Honestly, for someone who has lived her whole life in the North of Ireland where informing is...to put it mildly... frowned upon, it seems to be Clare's favourite pastime. I genuinely thought Fionnula might actually kill us all but it turned out she had something much more sinister in mind...she threatened to ban us from the chippy!!! Can you imagine? Luckily, Mammy was able to cut a deal. We clean the chip shop and all will be forgiven.

I mean, scrubbing down a greasy deep fat fryer is nobody's idea of an ideal Sunday (although it did get us out of Mass, which was something) but at least things can't get any worse.

24TH OCTOBER

So we sort of set fire to Fionnula's curtains and almost burned down the chip shop. Mammy tried to blame it on the IRA but that didn't wash. We're banned from the chip shop indefinitely and have to pay for the damage. Ironically, we are really going to need those jobs now.

Aunt Sarah went on the UTV news at six to talk about Uncle Colm's kidnapping or whatever it was. She looked really well and the producer said she was a natural. They asked her if she fancied presenting a mid-morning slot but it would have meant giving up her job as a beautician, which she considers her calling, so she turned them down.

25th October

We all start our jobs this weekend. Clare's going to tutor a little girl who's sitting her eleven plus soon — I mean, I could do it in my sleep but Clare was keen so I thought I'd let her have the opportunity. Michelle's gonna do a bit of babysitting — the child will be sleeping so that's a pretty cushy number. Orla's got a dog-walking position — she's good with animals — she's probably better with animals than she is with people, actually. James is gonna do some gardening and I'm starting a car valet service — I mean, I've only got one client booked so far but I've made some business cards so I think it's really gonna take off. I'll probably need to employ some staff soon. Then, I'll just be overseeing things. Oh maybe I could employ the others. That would be a really nice gesture. Then again, that could be a bit awkward...being their boss and being their friend. Nepotism probably isn't a good look for a new company either. Yeah, I'm gonna have to give this some thought.

(Note to self: double-check the meaning of nepotism.)

D.I.C.C.S.

Derry's Immaculate Car Cleaning Service

No job too big.

No job too small.

D.I.C.C.S. will tackle them all.

Call D.I.C.C.S. on Derry 229612 and our
Manager Ms Erin Quinn will
give you a quote today.

30TH OCTOBER

We've all been sacked! It's totally unfair. Clare went round to tutor

the ten-year-old only to discover she was some sort of rain wain* –

like, there's a rumour she's a member of Mensa. Clare was struggling

to keep up and, in the end, the mother saw through her. Michelle's

babysitting started well enough; this young couple were going on their

first night out since their six-month-old was born. The Mammy told

Michelle to go into the nursery and take a peek at the wee man while

she finished getting ready. Michelle peered into the cot and said out

loud, "Christ, you're not much to look at, are you, son?" not banking on the fact that there was a monitor in the room – the ma heard every word so that was pretty much the end of that. James, it turns out, is a really gifted gardener. Unfortunately, he chopped down a tree in the garden next door to the one he was supposed to be working in. Which nobody was buzzing* about. Orla was tasked with taking four Jack Russell terriers for a walk, and for some reason she thought it would be a good idea to return them to their owners kitted out in children's clothes. They weren't impressed. I rocked up at this swanky house ready to wash the BMW sitting in the drive – moments later Jenny Joyce comes out – I could have died! It was her house, her dad's car and now I was basically their servant. She pulled up a patio chair and started critiquing my work. I tried to remain dignified and professional, but she was being a total bitch and eventually one thing led to another and I accidentally tipped a bucket of water over her. So now we are all jobless and skint. Our parents are going to have to foot the bill for the damage to Fionnula's – they've said they're going to be deducting the cost from our student loans when we go to university. But I've heard the student loan is absolutely massive...like, apparently you couldn't spend it all if you tried, so I'm not that bothered really.

31st OCTOBER

Halloween. The biggest night of the year in Derry and we're grounded!

Just because we accidentally set fire to a chip shop and couldn't pay for the damage. I spent months making that 'Alice in Wonderland' costume and Orla was all set to be the Mad Hatter — it's just **SO UNFAIR!**

1st November

I saw David Donnelly on the bus today. Things have been so awkward between us since I didn't turn up for his gig. He's doing this really weird thing of not talking about it — acting like he didn't even notice or something. It obviously really hurt him. I'm in such a difficult position because it's impossible to explain why I didn't show up — the whole nun murder thing...no, **NOT** nun murder — I mean, we didn't murder a nun — but it's, like, how do I even get into what happened that day without it sounding...well, mad?

My relationship with David reminds me a bit of Mulder and Scully...I mean, not the alien stuff...David doesn't believe in aliens...at least, I don't think he does. No, just in the sense that neither of us can really say how we feel. There's just too much at stake. Anyway, when he got off the bus, he dropped his ticket and I sort of took it...stole it? Is that wrong? I'm sure I'm overthinking things. I'm sure it's fine.

(The ticket didn't smell of anything except the Ulsterbus depot.)

4th November

School is totally stressing me out. It's just so much pressure. All this focus on exam performance — it's not good for me. I'm an artist. I need time to be creative. So I've had this brilliant idea. I'm going to go to Sister Michael and suggest I do a four-day week. That will give me some time to concentrate on my writing. She knows how talented I am. I'm sure she'll be fully onboard.

5th November

Sister Michael didn't go for the four-day week thing. Raging*. She said I have "work ethic issues as it stands", which is simply not true. I'm gonna knock my R.E. assignment out of the park now just to prove her wrong. Well, not right now. I mean I'm knackered. I need to ease myself in. Maybe I'll rent a video?

Pirate Pauline's Film Club

New Titles Now Available!

Forrest Gump
Tom Hanks is an eejit* who has to be in the middle of everything.

The Shawshank Redemption
Political prisoners could take a leaf out of Tim Robbins' book.
If you say you see this twist coming, you're talking balls.

Interview with the Vampire
Tom Cruise is a creepy wee shite. Then again, when is he not?
(All releases come with Korean subtitles at no extra cost.)

1st December

Stop Press!

RTÉ are having a 'Murder, She Wrote' marathon tonight. Four episodes back to back. I am buzzing*! I absolutely love 'Murder, She Wrote'. I can't imagine what it must be like to live in a small town with so much violent crime.

Okay, so Derry isn't the biggest and arguably has had its fair share of violent crime too but it's all Troubles related so that's different. Nobody ever gets killed by a fountain pen at a fancy dress party or anything. I often think if Jessica lived in the North of Ireland, she'd sort it all out. I mean, for someone who isn't even a member of the police force she has a pretty flawless record when it comes to catching the culprit.

But hold on...Is she maybe too good? Why's she always sticking her nose in? Is it odd that she knows someone involved in every single case? Is Jessica involved somehow? Is she covering for someone? Is she covering for herself? Are all these murders just research for her next mystery novel? Is Jessica Fletcher a psychopath? Oh my God, how has nobody put all these pieces together before?! Why am I cursed with this intellect?!

Jessica Fletcher isn't a psychopath. I'm being ridiculous.

Or am I?

I am.

I don't want to think about this anymore, it's hurting my brain.

3RD DECEMBER

The Christmas exams are coming up and I haven't done anything.
Well, that's not true. I've watched **A LOT** of 'Murder, She Wrote'. If
I fail these exams, my ma is gonna kill me. I'm gonna get stuck into the
revision right now.

4TH DECEMBER

Last night was just so productive. I worked out the entire cast list for
the eventual movie of this book. Claire Danes will play me. And I think
Jared Leto would make a perfect David Donnelly. They've already
worked closely together on 'My So-Called Life' so the chemistry's
there.

If Claire Danes isn't available, I think the girl who plays Libby in
'Neighbours' would also work.

Cast List for Movie of My Memoirs

Parts will be offered on the condition that their Derry accent is flawless.

Erin Quinn – Claire Danes/Libby from 'Neighbours'

David Donnelly – Jared Leto/David Duchovny

Mary Quinn – Melanie Griffith/Julie Goodyear

Gerry Quinn – Liam Neeson

Joe McCool – John Wayne (check he's alive)

Sarah McCool – Isabella Rossellini

Orla McCool – Jim Carrey

Clare Devlin – The one who plays Six on 'Blossom'

Michelle Mallon – Pamela Anderson (with hair dyed dark)

James Maguire – Spike from 'Press Gang'

Sister Michael – Robert De Niro

DERRYWOOD

5TH DECEMBER

Really need to do some studying tonight. This is a joke!

6TH DECEMBER

I did it! I finally wrote out **ALL** the lyrics to The Cranberries' 'No Need to Argue' album. Dolores is such a poet.

7th December

Jesus Christ, the exams are less than a week away and I still haven't done a tap! I am not lifting my head tonight.

8th December

HOW HAVE I STILL NOT DONE ANYTHING?! I spent three hours playing 'Stop The Bus' with Orla last night, which was a mistake because when it comes to 'Stop The Bus' Orla is undefeated.

9th December

Okay, so it's come to my attention that not everybody knows what 'Stop The Bus' is. The gang came round to study tonight and we thought we'd squeeze in a quick game when James informed us that they don't play it in England. Another example of the English lagging behind culturally, I guess. So because I don't want to confuse my international readership, I thought I'd better explain. Everyone takes a piece of paper and a pen. You begin with the letter A and must think of a girl's name, a boy's name, a place, an occupation, an animal, a song and a film title beginning with that letter. Whoever finishes first shouts 'Stop the bus' and wins the round. You proceed to work your way through the alphabet.

STOP THE BUS

Letter	Girl's Name	Boy's Name	Place	Occupation	Animal	Song	Film
A	Aine	Andrew	Australia	Astronaut	Anteater	All That She Wants	Ace Ventura
B	Bronagh	Brendan	Belgium	Bee-Keeper	Brontosaurus	Baby Come Back	Back to the Future
C	Clara	Colm	Coleraine	Colourist	Cat	Caribbean Blue	Cool Runnings

10th December

Oh my fucking God, why have I wasted two nights writing out the rules to 'Stop The Bus'??? The exams are **THREE DAYS AWAY!!!**

11th December

It's all going to be fine. James watched this documentary about subliminal messages and apparently if we sleep with our study notes under our pillow, the information will seep into our subconscious. I'm amazed this didn't occur to me before, actually. It's pretty obvious.

12th December

So James was talking balls! Slept on my study notes all night and all I have to show for it is a Biro mark on my forehead.

13th December

8am

Devastating news!

Toto is dead! I can't get my head around it. I loved that dog. Knocked down by an army Land Rover — it was no way to go. My poor Mammy saw it happen. I mean, her and Toto didn't see eye to eye a lot of the time, but she's really cut up about it. You don't know what you've got till it's gone, I suppose.

On a totally unrelated note — usually if someone at school has had a family bereavement they don't have to sit exams on compassionate grounds.

Dogs are technically part of the family — aren't they?

4pm

Sister Michael said dead dog or no dead dog I'm sitting the exams. There's only one thing for it — I'm gonna have to do an all-nighter. Will ring round the others later and see if they're up for it. If we all put our heads together, I really think we can pull it off.

Derry Journal

NING ED. 32 PAGES ESTABLISHED 1772 IRELAND 30P UK 40P

WICKED HOAX

A local group of students have been the creators of a cruel prank on their local Catholic church.

Noel Ahern

AN ELABORATE HOAX WAS created by a group of young students from Our Lady Immaculate College in Derry. Locals reported a story about a miracle observed in St Agnes's Catholic Church. The group of students in question were in the church early one morning praying to a statue of the Virgin Mary for good luck in their exams.

The group of students claimed to have seen the Virgin Mary's statue smirk at them, before she cried real tears. The incident was reported to local schoolteacher Sister Michael before being taken to a Catholic priest with some experience in these matters, Father Peter.

The priest described how the apparition had initially created a feeling of great excitement in the community due to the potential of the religious miracle. Visits to the church had picked up after the revelations, with particular devotion being shown to the statue of Our Lady of the Sorrows. Father Peter, who is now taking an extended sabbatical, said to the 'Derry Journal', "There is no excuse for anyone toying with the faith of devout Catholic men and women."

'The Journal' spoke to local shopkeeper Dennis O'Doherty, who said he was appalled by the incident, and described how one of the students had boasted about her special relationship with "Jesus's ma" and had convinced him to part with a large bag of pick 'n' mix free of charge, leaving Mr O'Doherty feeling he'd been "taken for a fool".

The students have now been named as Erin Quinn, Orla McCool, Clare Devlin, Michelle Mallon and James Maguire. They were unavailable for comment.

ERRY OOTBALL EAM ELEBRATES

on Grattan

HIS WEEK DERRY RNAL celebrate the versary of the foundation heir club. Local footballer t Forsythe recalls how far club has come and tells his erience of it: you never et your first big game. For 'hole generation of local ple September 8th 1985 't just mark the return of or football to the Derry, was the first opportunity xperience the adrenaline 1 of live sport at a packed und.

don't claim to have known it about what was going on en my father Francis took to the Brandywell as a six-r-old that day.

ut my memories of the

City's Irish League games with his grandfather Joefus in the 50s and early 60s and was keen to be back for the first big event in what was, in many ways, the biggest local theatre of them all.

There were lots of people too and not just in the cemetery, everywhere you looked there were boys precariously perched on lampposts, walls and roofs. He doesn't remember how he managed it but, when we went through the turnstiles, my daddy managed to blag us up into the Glentoran Stand.

As we walked up the wee staircase of the, even then, decrepit old stand, within a matter of seconds I cast my eyes on the pitch for the first time as my line of vision suddenly shifted from the back pockets of Lee and blue jeans to a glorious aerial view of the packed ground.

One of the last memories of my childhood is how often

he beat the rest of the Derry team by himself? Would they not let the team mascot play just for the first five minutes?"

Is it any wonder when I spotted myself in the brilliant "rushes" footage of the game uploaded by Vinny Cunningham that my da bought me an ice cream! A few things stand out when you watch those 17 minutes of video that UTV recorded that day.

First things first, it's not a myth, Derry men in the 80s really did all wear white socks, elasticated bomber jackets and thick moustaches.

There is almost an eerie atmosphere before the game as supporters quietly shuffle into the ground, there are very few wearing the team colours and there is no chanting – it's as if the wonderful football has been away so long that no one really knows what to do at all. I might not see much of the action, but I was more than willing to take my chances and as we walked towards the ground, I barely spoke as I took in the swarms of people making their towards the already packed ground. More, pg 6.

14th December

Okay, I take it most of you will have read the absolute hatchet job the 'Derry Journal' did on us. I'm considering suing for defamation of character. None of us can even leave our houses without getting harassed. Dennis the shopkeeper calls us "The Children of Fuckima", which doesn't even make sense. Like, that's not even a play on words. Absolute moron.

(Is there a chance Dennis might read this when it's published? Is it wise to call him a moron? Obviously, I want to remain true to myself as a writer and not censor my work but I am quite scared of him. Worth giving this some thought.)

The bottom line is we did not stage a fake miracle to get out of sitting our history exam. It was simply a series of unfortunate misunderstandings and I strongly believe Father Peter steered the truth to fit his own personal agenda. I mean, I'm not one for conspiracy theories but I'm wondering if the Pope told him to market Derry as the next Lourdes — there's a lot of money to be made out of these apparitions...when Granda went to Lourdes he came back with Our Lady of Lourdes bath towels, an ashtray, some T-shirts, pencil cases for me and Orla and a couple of Sacred Heart dummies for Baby Anna — honestly, Take That have less merchandise. Apparently, some people are saying I faked the miracle to impress Father Peter because I fancied him.

As if! I mean, he does have amazing hair but he's a priest! It's disgusting! Then again, people in this place don't tend to let the truth get in the way of a good story.

Apparitions and miracles index

Virgin Mary, apparition 74

  giving instructions to

    bless a spring 166

    build a chapel 168

    build a convent 171

    pick flowers 173

    pray 175

    produce medallions 178

    produce statue 181

  giving prophecy

    civil conflict, during a 94

    famine, during 97

    peacetime, during 82

    wartime, during 87

  giving secret 101

  giving gift 102

  healed from

    blindness 112

    chronic illness 114

    deafness 110

    paralysis 117

  resurrected

    cat 61

    dog 68

    lizard 69

    other 71

  seen by children only 76

  silent 77

  statue

    glowing 130

    weeping 140

  takes viewers on mystic journey 79

  transforms clothing 75

Weather, unexplained

  dry ground during rain 150

  golden light, intense 154

Weight gain, unexplained 161

It's difficult for me to explain what actually happened without telling the world what my ma did. And while I'm appalled by her actions, she's my mother. I have to protect her. So even though speaking out would vindicate me...my lips are sealed.

15th December

4pm

I cannot believe my mother has the audacity to start* me about the state of my bedroom. I mean, I'm sorry, Mary, but you lost any right you had to tell me off when you pretended my dog had been assassinated by the British Army and then gave him to Maureen Malarkey! All because he could never live up to the impossible standards of her childhood mutt Gypsy — who, by the way, wasn't even that cute! The cheek of the woman! My bedroom isn't untidy — I just have a very particular system that she doesn't understand.

I'm going round to Maureen Malarkey's right now and demanding she gives my Toto back. I will not keep my mother's dirty secret any longer!

4.30pm

Went round to Maureen's to get Toto but he refused to come with me. Wee Shite. He's on to a good thing there, you see, it turns out he has his own bedroom.

Oh, and Sister Michael is making us take the history exam we missed tomorrow. Really better do some revision now. I'll start the second 'Brookside' is over.

What's 4B? Leader of the campaign against the British in the
War of Independence?? Erin

No idea. James.

It was Mick Hucknall. Orla

He's the lead singer of Simply Red, Orla. *Erin*

So who's this hairdresser Father Peter ran off with? –

Michelle

Michael Collins. I think Clare

*The hairdresser is a **man!** James*

No – he led the campaign against the British...I think.
Clare

What an arsehole. Erin

He was actually a pretty important
Irish historical figure. Clare

Not Michael Collins, Father Peter! Erin

Look, let's stop this before we get caught. Clare

Our Lady Immaculate College

Tel: 0504 649 6412
Fax: 0504 649 6414

Dear Mr and Mrs Quinn,

I wish I didn't have to write this letter because...well, it's boring. Erin and several other students were caught cheating in their Irish History resit this afternoon. She will now have to resit the resit.

I pity you both.

Regards,

Sr. Michael

Sr Michael

Principal

Directors: Father John O'Brien, Cllr. Michael Kennedy, Mr. Conor McCarthy, Mrs. Aoife Moore. Registered in Belfast. Company No. 8769521

18th December

I can't believe it's almost Christmas! Orla's saying she's not celebrating it this year — she's still cut up about not getting that job as an elf in Santa's Grotto. Apparently, she was too tall, which, to be fair, is discrimination. I've never seen her this upset. She doesn't even want to watch 'The Late Late Toy Show'* tonight. I bet she will.

Merry Christmas

Dear Joe, Mary, Sarah, Gerry, Erin, Orla and Anna,

Uncle Colm here. Wishing you a Merry Christmas.

Although I'll be seeing you all on the day itself so it might make more sense to wish you a Merry Christmas then, in the flesh so to speak. Now, in saying that, there's no harm in me doing it twice, I suppose. Nobody ever died from someone wishing them a Merry Christmas too many times. At least, not as far as I know now. I haven't looked into it. So maybe I shouldn't speak out of turn.

I'll probably be with you at around 3pm. I think I'll head to the 12 o'clock Mass for it's always a good length. Then I'll do the rounds up at the cemetery — which takes the guts of two hours. The other day I says to myself, I says, Colm, you know more dead people these days than you do living. It's desperate altogether — they're dropping like flies so they are. But at least we're all still here. God bless us and save us. Sure, we can't complain. I was just saying to Maggie McKeogh, you know Maggie? Worked up at the shirt factory there? Sewed her two fingers together back in 1985? Lovely woman...anyway I says to her I says Maggie... (P.T.O.)

24th December

It's Christmas Eve! So excited! Really hope I get the computer for my main present. I mean, it's sort of ridiculous that I had to put it on my Christmas list in the first place. I'm sick of saying it's a **NECESSITY.** My mammy usually puts together a little stocking for me and Orla as well – just full of wee novelty things, chocolate money, sweetie cigarettes, stick-on tattoos, really stupid stuff. I've told her not to bother this year – we're sixteen...we're not wains*...it's embarrassing.

25th December

5am

I will never get over this. Christmas Day and I wake up to **NO STOCKING!** This is **BULLSHIT!** My ma has just tried to play the whole "But you said you didn't want one" card. She never listens to anything I say, usually...why's she suddenly interested in my feelings now? **OBVIOUSLY,** I wanted one. This has ruined Christmas.

8am

Now Mammy's saying I'm not allowed to open my main present until after Mass. This is actual child abuse! At least I can wear my new

Christmas outfit. I got this really cute little navy pinafore with knee-high socks – it's very 'Saved by the Bell'. I hope David Donnelly's at Mass. If he is, I'm definitely going to go up for Communion so he gets to see how cracker* I look.

10am

Orla just came round and she's wearing the **EXACT SAME OUTFIT.** Obviously, Mammy and Aunt Sarah got some sort of two-for-one deal in the catalogue. This is mortifying. I'm gonna have to keep my coat on. No Body of Christ for me this morning, thank you very much.

1pm

Mass is over. Thanks be to God, David Donnelly was a no-show. He's probably an atheist – Christ, he's so cool. I wanted to be an atheist but my ma wouldn't let me. I don't get what the big deal is. I mean, I'm sure they still get into heaven when they die. Finally was allowed to open my main present. It was a word processer, which, to be fair, is probably even better than a computer. It's more compact so I'll be able to take it to meetings with me and stuff. Orla got a New York Knicks top – she's been really into them ever since we watched an episode of 'Seinfeld' where they go to a basketball game. Granda got a foot spa – I've never seen a man so buzzing*. My wee sister Anna probably did the best – the living room's like a toy shop. But it's all just boring baby stuff. Uncle Colm's coming round for dinner soon. Lord help us all.

3pm

Me and Orla just spent the last hour playing with Anna's Interactive Care Bear — it is beyond class*. Then Anna started crying and my ma made us give it back to her. They have that wain* ruined*.

4pm

Uncle Colm just launched into a monologue about why he prefers chicken to turkey and I'm convinced I blacked out for fifteen minutes. The gang are all on their way round. Can't wait to see what they got.

7pm

Clare got this massive arts and crafts set — it means she can make hairbands and friendship bracelets. So we all know what we'll be getting as birthday presents for the foreseeable. James got a leather jacket, it's awful — he looks like a T-Bird. Michelle wanted a Wonderbra but, let's face it, that was never gonna happen. She got a sovereign ring — she's really into it but I think it's a bit tacky, personally. We also did something very clever — we all asked for different CDs, which means we can swap them round and make mix tapes for each other, etc. — there's no flies on us. My da lost the will to live and started feeding Uncle Colm whiskey. It turns out he's much more interesting when he's blocked*.

✳ CHRISTMAS MIX TAPE MADNESS! ✳

—— x ——

(Sadly, none of us were allowed a Nirvana CD
as our mas think they're a cult.)

1. 'All That She Wants' – Ace of Base

2. 'Insane in the Brain' – Cypress Hill

3. 'Pray' – Take That

4. 'Mr Loverman' – Shabba Ranks

5. 'Waterfalls' – TLC

6. 'Let's Talk About Sex' – Salt-N-Pepa

7. 'Back For Good' – Take That

8. 'Informer' – Snow

9. 'My Lovin'' – En Vogue

10. 'Sure' – Take That

11. 'The Key, The Secret' – Urban Cookie Collective

12. 'Deeply Dippy' – Right Said Fred

13. 'Stay' – East 17

14. 'I Will Always Love You' – Whitney Houston (Clare made us)

15. 'Rock 'n' Roll Star' – Oasis (James pretends to like them)

16. 'The Macarena' – Los de Rio

1st JANUARY

Here are my New Year's resolutions:

1. Get an agent. Obviously, when this book is finished, I'm gonna be in demand but it's important to find the right person to represent me. Artists like myself are difficult, temperamental, intense. It's vital the agent understands what they're taking on.

2. Similarly, I need to find a publishing house who 'get' my creative vision. Who won't try to limit me or put me in a box. I'll be writing in many genres...literary, horror, romance, comedy, children's fiction...I need someone who can keep up.

3. Get a nose piercing.

2ND JANUARY

My ma said under no circumstances am I getting a nose piercing.

7tH JANUARY

Huge News! The trampy colourist from Hair 'n' Flair has **DUMPED FATHER PETER!!!** He shaved his head and she was furious, apparently. To be fair to her, it does nothing for him. Wonder what he'll do now? There can't be many options for an ex-priest with a shaved head. Maybe he'll become a monk?

Parish Bulletin:

The Derry Diocese is gearing up for its annual "Children of Chernobyl" visit. If your family are interested in hosting one of these wonderful young people, please arrange an appointment with Father Conway at St Agnes's parochial house.

Make enquiries early to avoid disappointment - unfortunately we have a limited number of Ukrainians this year and demand is typically very high.

14TH JANUARY

Yes! My ma is letting me have a Ukrainian! We have to go to the parochial house today and pick one. I'm assuming they're all in some sort of catalogue and you just choose the one you like the look of.

15TH JANUARY

So we didn't get to choose. Father Conway chose for us. Mine is called Katya. Of course, Jenny Joyce was there. She asked for three Ukrainians, but Father Conway was very clear — one Ukrainian per person. Serves her right. Greedy bitch.

I'm going to write to Katya to introduce myself. I just need to make sure I strike the right tone. She'll probably be a bit intimidated about visiting somewhere as metropolitan as Derry. I don't want to overwhelm her. I might have to play it all down a bit.

Dear Katya,

I am writing to introduce myself. My name is Erin Quinn. I am an award-winning writer from Derry, Northern Ireland and I will be your host for the duration of your stay here. I am acutely aware that coming here will be a huge culture shock for you. But worry not, I shall explain everything and be by your side at all times. I've travelled a lot, having spent many summers in Buncrana*, Bundoran and Portnoo, to name but a few, so I'm well versed in communicating with people less sophisticated than those in my home city. If you have any questions at all, please do not hesitate to ask. I look forward to hearing from you.

Best wishes

Erin Quinn

PS I have included one of my poems, 'Crossfire Child' – the meaning of which will be difficult for you to grasp but I'm sure you can still appreciate the rhythm of the language.

I get letters you write, but will not reply. I see you on visit, is enough.

Katya

Erin Quinn

Our Lady Immaculate College

Derry

16TH JANUARY

I think Katya's English maybe isn't the best. I'm sure they don't have much of an education system over there with everything that's happened. I think I'm going to have to simplify my correspondence to her.

Dear Katya,

Below is a complete and cohesive document outlining your itinerary
for the duration of your sojourn:

Sunday
Recitation of my poetry while exploring Derry's famous city walls.

Monday
A read-through of my play 'Julie and Ryan'. This will help you get
to grips with the human side of Northern Ireland's political conflict.

Tuesday
I've sort of had to say we'll meet up with my friends, although
maybe you'd rather spend all of your time on your own with me?
We will probably have established a special bond by now.

Thursday
Write a poem together about how my friendship and this
experience has changed your perspective on life and given
you hope for the future.

Friday
Return home. It will be difficult for you to leave me,
but I shall write.

30th JANUARY

The feud between Granda and Maureen Malarkey continues. She's still accusing him of stealing her baking tray, which he fervently denies. This led her to leave their pub quiz team, "The Bingo Wings", in protest — taking several of their smartest members with her. She's now formed a rival pub quiz team: "The Real Bingo Wings". Granda is absolutely fuming. Jim across the road feels very caught in the middle. He's trying to negotiate a Peace Deal but let's just say he's no John Hume*.

4th FEBRUARY

Really starting to feel this chip shop ban now but Fionnula will not be moved on the matter. There's only so much pizza a girl can eat. It's funny, I never get sick of chips. I wonder if it's because of the potato famine? Like, now Irish people take their potato products whenever they can get them, no questions asked. Like, maybe it's in our DNA to crave chips. I definitely think there's something in this. Perhaps I should do some research.

Can't do research as banned from chip shop. Fionnula is stalling science now!

7TH FEBRUARY

Oh my God, I was tidying my room (Mammy said if I didn't do it she'd do it for me — which I've learned from experience translates as "turf everything I own into the front street"), when I found this balled-up piece of paper behind my desk. I unfurled it (fancy term for opened it up) and discovered it was a letter James had written to his friend in London. It must have fallen from his bag when he was last round here. His insight into Derry life is absolutely fascinating. Completely wrong but fascinating all the same. I started wondering if this would be an interesting addition to these memoirs — an outsider's perspective. I suppose I should ask his permission to include it...but I'm worried he won't let me. Anyway, if he takes issue with it, I can just pay him off. I'm going to be a millionaire when this thing is published.

Dear John,

Thanks for writing. It was so good to hear from you.
Derry is a pretty strange place, to be honest. When I first
arrived, I thought everybody I encountered was having an
argument, but it turns out that's just how they speak.
They seem to survive solely on a diet of carbohydrates and
they're all obsessed with walls. They're also pretty pissed off
with the English and they keep talking about some guy
called Wayne, who I haven't met yet. They describe everything
as 'wee', even things that are actually quite big — it's a bit
confusing. Anyway, I'm sure it won't be too long till I see you.
Mum is probably going to come and get me any minute now.
She's been really busy with her new swimsuit range, but
she's launching it soon so then things should get back to
normality.

Can't wait to get back home and see all the lads.

All the best,

James

PS Could you please send me some vitamin tablets with your
next letter? I think I'm getting scurvy.

14TH FEBRUARY

8.15am

I got a Valentine's card! Oh my God, I'm actually shaking! It's a Forever Friends one. Two teddy bears holding a heart — so lovely! Inside there's a message: "I think about you every day. The problem is I'm too shy to say. Love ???"

I mean, it's obviously David Donnelly. He's in a band and that could be the chorus of a love ballad. I can't wait to tell him I feel the same.

for my
valentine

I think about you every day.

The problem is I'm too shy to say.

Love ???

4.30pm

So at break time Clare, Orla and James produce the exact same Valentine's card with the exact same message. Michelle sent them. She couldn't breathe for laughing. She's so immature.

20th FEBRUARY

11am

They're here! The Ukrainians are here! We have to go to Mass to collect them. Christ, but I hope my Ukrainian is better than Jenny's Ukrainian.

2pm

So Katya is upstairs settling in. I think she's finding it all a bit much, the critter*. The English barrier is proving to be a bit of a problem. To give you a quick example, she described my letters as "boring" when she obviously meant "challenging". She also told James he was hot, then, embarrassed by her mistake, doubled down and snogged him. I think she's just trying really hard to impress us all, which I guess is understandable. She's also pretty confused by the political situation here – she seems to think Catholics and Protestants are the same. I have **A LOT** of work to do. I'm gonna take her to the Derry walls later. They will blow her mind!

5pm

Katya wasn't that into the walls.

Almost teatime. We're having traditional Irish stew to welcome Katya.
Well, I say traditional, but in Derry we use mince instead of lamb.
Nobody's ever been able to give me a satisfactory explanation as to why.
I've come to the conclusion that – like most things in Derry – we do it
because it's cheaper.

Mary's Derry Stew

Ingredients

Half a pound of Doherty's special mince* rolled into bite-sized balls

1 onion cut up into wile* wee pieces

A whack* of spuds, peeled and quartered

3 carrots, chopped

Bisto instant gravy granules

Method

1. Heat a drop of oil in the big pot.
2. Add the Doherty's meatballs and fry the life out of them.
3. Add the onions. Fry until they soften.
4. Remove meatballs and onions and set aside.
5. Put the spuds and carrots into the big pot and cover with water.
6. Place lid on the big pot and boil until the carrots are squealing for mercy.
7. Turn down heat.
8. Put two or three spoons of Bisto in the wee jar. Add boiling water. Stir.
9. Add gravy to the big pot and bung in the meatballs and onions.
10. Stir with wooden spoon until thickened.
11. Bowl up and absolutely clatter* with HP Brown Sauce.
12. Serve with thickly cut slices of lodger's loaf dripping in butter.
    Preferably kerrygold.

8pm

Scandal! Scandal! Major scandal! Granda has a girlfriend! Boke*. Boke. Bokeorama*. He's been tucking into cream horns with a trampy widow on Pump Street. Granny will be turning in her grave. Men – they're all the same. You can't even die safe in the knowledge that their head won't be turned by some hussy before the decade's out. Maeve, her name is. He met her at the Stations of the Cross in St Agnes's. Honestly, that chapel's like club 18 to 30. We're all thoroughly disgusted. Well, except Katya, who didn't seem to know what was going on.

Granda Joe's top three Stations of the Cross
in no particular order

1. Jesus falls for the second time.
2. Simon gives Jesus a hand with the cross.
3. Jesus meets the women of Jerusalem.

Jesus is the light

(at the end of my cigarette)

THE BEST BUNS IN DERRY ①

1. The undisputed Bun Champion. The Bap. Filling and versatile. Plain bap, toasted bap, crisp bap, chip buttie bap — the possibilities are endless. A staple of any proud Derry native's diet.

2. The Gravy Ring. No bun run is complete without a couple of gravy rings. Basically, a doughnut rolled in a bag of sugar.

3. The Turnover. A diamond-shaped pastry clattered with icing.

4. The Cream Finger. A finger bun slit down the middle and packed with cream and a wee bit of jam.

5. The Cream Horn. A flaky puff pastry in the shape of a horn filled with cream. A challenge to eat but worth the effort.

21st February

6pm

Katya is really starting to get on my nerves. I just don't really think she's being very appreciative of everything I'm trying to do for her. And Clare is just so up her hole* at the minute. (Note to self: find a more eloquent way of saying "up her hole".) She's trying so hard to impress her — she's gone all Martin Luther King on it. Also Katya and James now seem to be somehow going out? What the hell is she up to? I just do not trust her. There's absolutely no way she could fancy him. He's all English and...curly. There's something funny going on and I intend to get to the bottom of it.

Oh, and we were in the cafe earlier when Jenny rocked in with her Ukrainian Artem, who seems absolutely cracker*. I thought about asking if I could trade Katya for him but decided against it. I think she's quite attached to him. Well, she's literally attached to him...with a rope. Apparently, he kept running off so it makes sense, I suppose. Michelle really fancies him and I do think they would make a good couple. I think the fact that he doesn't understand a word that she's saying could be a positive thing.

Jenny's decided to have a big welcome party for all the Ukrainians at her place tonight. Which I actually think is a really good idea. It would be nice for them to get together — it might make them feel a bit more at home. So I'm willing to put my many, many issues with Jenny to one side on this occasion for the greater good.

Oh, and just as a random, unimportant aside, David Donnelly is going to be there. He's DJing. He so talented, it's insane. Better get ready, I suppose! Might wear the choker Clare made me. That arts and crafts set she got for Christmas was money well spent.

you're invited!

★ PARTY!

Hey guys! I'm having a Party!
Date: 21st Feb.
Venue: My Place (Address overleaf)
Dress Code: ukrainian chic
Kick off time: 7.30pm
we'll be moving and grooving to
MC David Donnelly's top disco tunes!
Be there or be square!

(Chupa Chups on a first come,
first served basis.)

Is he Boyfriend Material?

Take this questionnaire to find out if he really is for you.

1 When you see him you:

A. Find it hard to make eye contact and talk sensibly – he makes you feel all wobbly inside

B. Find it hard to get a chance to talk to him – he's always with a group of his friends

C. Could talk to him for hours – he's just like a friend, but better

2 You're going to the same event. In your dreams does he:

A. Nod at you from across the room, but you can sense his eyes on you all night

B. Break away from the lads to give you a hug and a kiss on the cheek

C. Meet you beforehand and you come together

3 Do you guys have the same taste in music and film?

A. He's very into his arts, but we don't really talk about them, just smoulder

B. Yes, we met at our shared hobby group but it's the only thing we have in common

C. Not really, but we love to hang out and argue for hours about who's wrong or right

4 Do you guys have an in-joke?

A. We totally would, we just don't know each other well enough yet

B. All his jokes are with his friends – but that's okay, right?

C. So many – we laugh all the time at the silliest things

5 You bump into him when you're out with no makeup on. Do you:

A. Freak out: he's never seen you before without a carefully planned look

B. Dive into the toilets and put some lip gloss and mascara on – you always have it with you just in case

C. Do nothing – you're so comfortable with each other that you don't care if he sees you with no makeup on

6 You've had a bad day at school. What does he do to cheer you up?

A. Nothing – you guys don't talk enough yet to share the negative things

B. He tries to make you laugh by telling you funny stories about what the lads got up to that day

C. He says nothing but will happily watch silly movies with you and listen to you moan

If you answered:

Mostly A's

He's the artistic loner you're in love with from a distance. You might make a good couple – but you'll probably never know as you can't get close enough to find out. Maybe it's time to ask yourself if you're addicted to the chase?

Mostly B's

He's the fun-loving centre of his social gang. You guys have a great time together, but you sometimes wonder if his friends are more important to him than you are.

Mostly C's

He's a good friend who knows you at your best – and worst. Maybe it's time you saw him in a new way! Before you know it, friendship could turn to L.O.V.E.

Erin,

I know you told me I'm not allowed to pass notes under the door when you're in the bath, but this is urgent!!! I need advice about my outfit for Jenny's party. Do you think my trainers will fit in her chocolate fountain??? If not, I'm gonna have to wear my wee pumps.

Orla

7pm

Sweet and gentle Jesus Christ! I just accidentally peeked inside Katya's bag only to discover a packet of condoms. Actual condoms. Sex condoms. Condoms that you use for sex. I knew she was up to something. She's planning to deflower James because she's a sicko who gets her kicks from corrupting innocent young men. And there is **NO WAY** James is allowed to have sex before me! I'd never live it down. I have to put a stop to this! Shit, better go, Granda's giving us a lift to Jenny's and he's calling me. To be continued...

22ND FEBRUARY

Okay, let's just get one thing straight. I did not call Katya a prostitute.
I am, like, 95 per cent certain I never uttered those words. The whole
thing has just been blown way out of proportion. Basically Katya refused
to come home with me and Jenny is now saying she's keeping her! My
Ukrainian! It's outrageous but because it's transpired that Artem was
not in fact a child from Chernobyl at all but a wee Protestant lad called
Clive, who took a wrong turn at Aldergrove airport, it means Jenny has
technically stuck to her quota of one Ukrainian per person. So legally
she hasn't done anything wrong but morally, well, I consider it theft.

Despite my misunderstanding with Katya (as I say, I'm 80 per cent positive I didn't call her a prostitute), there is no way she could like Jenny better than me. Her head's just been turned by Jenny's ridiculously massive house. God, but she's so shallow. Anyway, at least she didn't get round to sexing James. He's still not speaking to me about the fact that I "ruined" his "big chance". I'm the one who should be pissed off with him. I was so focused on defending his honour that I passed up David Donnelly's offer of a beer, which would have **DEFINITELY** led to him asking me out. James is soooooo selfish. Clare and her da have now safely returned Artem/Clive to his home in East Belfast. She was the only one he trusted because she spent the night prancing about in a top she could have bought from an Orange Order* stall on the twelfth. But look, with a bit of distance, I can now see that Katya and I were just not a good match. There's no hard feelings. I wish her well.

Katya,

How the hell could you do this to me? How could you betray me like this? I invite you into my home and you dump me for **JENNY JOYCE!** Well, I hope you're very happy together. You deserve each other. I will never forgive you for this! Ever!

Goodbye.

It's Erin, by the way.

Katya,

I'm sorry for my previous letter. I was upset. Please come back. I'll change.

I promise. I miss you.

Erin

B.F.F.
(sort of)

THE 'SATURDAY NIGHT' DANCE

1. Clap your hands in the air.

2. Move your arms to the right, then the left in a wave-like motion.

3. Step left leg out, step right leg out. Grab right elbow by left hand, twirl right arm. Repeat with left arm.

4. Roll your arms round each other as you bend forward, then stand straight again.

5. Put your right hand just above your right knee, then your left hand just above your left knee.

6. Put your right hand on your right arse cheek, then your left hand on your left arse cheek.

7. With your hands still on your arse, jump forward and then back.

8. Jump and turn clockwise.

9. Clap and repeat the moves.

28TH FEBRUARY

Have my eye on a really cracker* pair of ankle boots. I wonder if I can convince Mammy to part with £15 for them.

29TH FEBRUARY

Mammy said she will give me half the money. Which I guess means I can buy one ankle boot.

30TH FEBRUARY

Christ, but I'm so bored today. Hold on a minute. There is no 30th February. Shit...I must have gone wrong somewhere.

Jenny is kind, sweet girl.
You are bad person.
And shit poet.
Do not contact me again.

Katya

Erin Quinn

Our Lady Immaculate College

Derry

листівка

17th MARCH

11am

St Patrick's Day! Me and the gang are gonna go to the Music room and learn 'Riverdance'.

12pm

So Sister Michael walked in just as Clare fell through the drum kit.

18th MARCH

Detention.

19th MARCH

Detention.

20th MARCH

Detention.

21st MARCH

Detention.

9th APRIL

7.30am

Eugh, report cards today. I'm gonna have to get downstairs before Mammy and intercept it.

8am

My ma was waiting for the postman, like, since the crack of dawn. I never stood a chance.

OUR LADY IMMACULATE COLLEGE

REPORT CARD

PUPIL: **Erin Quinn**

SUBJECT	GRADE			
Maths	D			
Religious Education	B			
French	D			
Geography	B			
History	B			
Science	D			
English Language	B-			
English Literature	B+			
Irish	C			

TEACHER'S REPORT

A fairly disappointing term for Miss Quinn.

I appreciate she feels the Western Education and Library Board's syllabus is "limited" and "pedestrian", however, the fact that she still has to learn it remains.

Erin needs to develop and stick to a proper study schedule – asking her grandfather to "light a candle" at Mass isn't sufficient exam preparation.

Though I will say her attempts to memorise the entire curriculum the night before the exam displayed a level of optimism that was admirable.

I expect to see much improvement next term.

Sr. Michael

10TH APRIL

Grounded.

11TH APRIL

Grounded.

12TH APRIL

Grounded.

13TH APRIL

Grounded.

14TH APRIL

This is ridiculous. I'm an adult. I'm telling Mammy I'm going round to Michelle's – what's she gonna do?

15TH APRIL

Grounded indefinitely.

30TH APRIL

I saw David Donnelly at Dennis's shop today. He was being really weird. I tried to talk to him, but he just cut me off. He said he thought I was totally lousy. That what I called Katya at Jenny Joyce's party was really out of order. (I mean, I'm 75 per cent certain I did not call her a prostitute.) Of course I know what's really going on here. He's hurt. He thinks I rejected him, but he can't admit that. Stupid male pride. He'll come round.

I also think Dennis might have been drunk. He was singing Neil Diamond's 'Cracklin' Rosie'. He doesn't have a bad voice, actually.

THE RULES OF DENNIS'S WEE SHOP

1. DO NOT PISS ME OFF.

2. READ RULE ONE OVER AND OVER AGAIN UNTIL IT SINKS INTO YOUR THICK SKULL.

3. DON'T ASK FOR CREDIT.

4. YOU TOUCH IT, YOU BUY IT.

1st MAY

9am

The Orange Order* are having a practice run for their 12th July parade. Which is Zero Craic*, unless you enjoy rioting. Mammy has ordered us to pack up. We're heading to the caravan in Portnoo until things settle down.

Mary's Portnoo Packing List

Egg timer	Clothes pegs
Jim's telescope	Dustpan and brush
Mouse trap	1,000 piece jigsaw
Bandages	The big map
Windbreak	The wee map
Tea towels	The big spade
Hats	The wee spade
'RTÉ Guide'	Cluedo
St Christopher	Lilo
Teapot	Potty
Laundry basket	The wee bin
Batteries AAA and up	Rope
'Yellow Pages'	Wooden spoon
The bag of carrier bags	The big clock
Cling film	Bucket and spade
Roller skates	Bicycle
Extension lead	Poncho
Apples that need eating	Nail polish remover
Calor-gas camping stove	Catechism
Family photo album	Mop
Breadknife	The phone
The calculator	Punt* purse
Saw/hammer	
The rotating washing line	
Whiskey	

11am

Christ, the Orangemen are really going for it now. That Lambeg drum is certainly being given a thrashing. Quite envious of Jim across the road's double glazing.

I love Portnoo. It's this wee Donegal village on a great big beach, all white sand and green headlands and long walks. We'll stop off for a pint of Guinness (a glass of Football Special* for me and Orla) and some Taytos en route. I'll have cheese and onion because I'm normal. Orla goes for prawn cocktail — boke*. She only does it for attention.

I'm looking forward to some peace and quiet. I really need to focus on my new supernatural thriller 'Presence of the Past' (such a clever title). It'll be good to have a bit of a break from the gang, to be honest. They just don't understand the fact that my work is always my priority, their minor dramas but an insignificant distraction.

11.30am

The gang are coming to Portnoo with us. Happy Days! Granda is now insisting we bring the TV and video machine so he can watch 'Sleeping with the Enemy'.

4TH MAY

So Portnoo was pretty uneventful. Oh, actually that's not true.
Something really awful happened. We're all still a bit shaken up by
it. We lost Jim across the road's second-best tent! Well, I say lost.
The Provo* who was hiding in our boot stole it. We're not sure at what
point the Provo* got into the boot. Though, to be fair, we were all pretty
distracted by the fact that Granda Joe drove straight through a police
barricade and directly into the middle of the Orange March itself –
which is no place for a load of Catholics. Trust me. Daddy managed
to get us out of there by pretending to be a tourist. There's still some
debate over what accent he was supposed to be doing.

Video Village `VIDEO RENTAL` ▶

Every month Video Village asks one of its customers to review their favourite film.
Below Joe McCool, originally from Creggan, tells us why he loves 'Sleeping with the Enemy'.

'Sleeping with the Enemy' tells the story of this poor girl who marries an abusive arsehole that's obsessed with his tea towels. She can't take his abuse anymore and decides to fake her own death and assume a new identity, and you couldn't blame the critter* for as I say, the fella is a bad article. Anyway, she's going about her life in a different town with a different name and she meets this new lad who she thinks is great, but to be honest he's a bit of a drip. I think her standards are just really low because she was with arsehole features for so long. Eventually, arsehole features tracks her down. He causes all sorts of bother but in the end....and this is the best bit....she kills him. I love 'Sleeping with the Enemy' because your woman Julia Roberts is a great actress and also women killing men who are arseholes is my favourite genre of movie. I thoroughly recommend.

Joe McCool

113

Anyway, as soon as we discovered Provo* Emmett (not his real name) in the boot, it became clear he had his heart set on us driving him over the border. I guess because he was on the run or whatever. We stopped in Peggy's Diner to discuss the matter. Nobody could agree on the best course of action. Granda thought we should take him. Daddy didn't. Mammy and Aunt Sarah were on the fence. Orla was...well, on another planet. Anyway, Emmett (not his real name) either got fed up waiting or was made so uncomfortable by Michelle's aggressive 'flirting' that he decided to clear off, taking Jim's tent with him and leaving us to pay for his full Irish.

No tent obviously meant conditions in the caravan were cramped! It rained the whole weekend. Michelle was pissed off because she couldn't

go looking for boys. Orla was pissed off because she couldn't go looking for cheetahs. Clare finished 'Moby Dick' — she said she was disappointed there wasn't a bigger twist. James was asking a lot of questions about the IRA* and the UDA* and the RUC* — God, but we really do enjoy an acronym in this neck of the woods. Aunt Sarah gave everyone tarot card readings, which passed the time, but despite her "psychic certificate", she most certainly does not have a gift. She told me I was going to be a TV writer! I don't think so, somehow. I'm a poet, a playwright. TV's just broad vulgar entertainment. It's not art. I'm an artist.

Oh, Mammy thinks Provo* Emmett (not his real name) might also have nicked her punt* purse. I'm not so sure. She's forever losing that thing.

KNIGHT of WANDS.

THE MAGICIAN.

THE TOWER.

Certificate of Completion

This is to certify that

Sarah McCool

has completed
Psychic Studies level 1 – Tarot Cards Reading
Grade
Pass with Distinction

Portnoo

Dear Jim,
We're having a great time here in Portnoo. Hope the double glazing is keeping that aul' racket out. Thanks so much for the tent again. It's brilliant. I can see why it's your second best. Just out of interest, where did you buy it and how much did it cost?
Best, Joe

6TH MAY

So, after a lot of careful consideration, I've decided to write a television series. Despite my reservations about the medium, it does reach millions of people, and I've been blessed or maybe cursed with the voice of my generation. The masses deserve to hear it. To learn from it.
To be moved by it.

Mammy said we're allowed Viennetta tonight! Yes!!!

TV SHOW IDEAS!!!

1. 'Top of the Morning To You'-A show subverting Irish stereotypes? Everybody is really clever and teetotal???

2. 'Wink Murder'-What if someone could actually commit murder just by winking?

3. 'Leaper'-A guy time travels by leaping into the body of someone from the past in order to stop history taking the wrong course.

4. 'Original Sin'-A priest and a nun start a secret love affair. Period drama??

Shit. I just realised number 3 is basically 'Quantum Leap'.

15TH MAY

THE BETRAYAL!!!! So I just found out that David Donnelly has a GIRLFRIEND! It gets worse.

That girlfriend is none other than...
KATYA!!!! Yes, Katya the Ukrainian! The same Katya I invited into my home and treated like my sister! I'm broken. I'm inconsolable. Apparently, after we left Jenny Joyce's party, they got off with each other. They've been having a long-distance relationship ever since she went home. He's going to visit her next month.
They are both DEAD TO ME!

Book Launch Invite List
updated
again

1. ~~David Donnelly-Date~~. Banned. Two-timing prick.
   ~~We will definitely be going out by then.~~
2. ~~Mammy~~ Now banned as she
   clearly doesn't believe in me.
3. ~~Daddy~~ Banned, never stands up to Mammy.
4. ~~Granda~~ Banned, eating cream horns with tramps
   on Pump Street.
5. ~~Aunt Sarah~~ Banned, wouldn't lend me
   her heated rollers.
6. ~~Cousin Orla (Mammy will make me)~~ Banned
7. ~~Baby Anna~~ Banned   —no respect for
   cries too much.   personal boundaries.
8. ~~Clare Devlin (BF)~~ Banned. Is grass.
9. ~~Michelle Mallon (Joint BF)~~ Banned. Is liability.
10. ~~Jenny Joyce (For making her jealous reasons)~~
    Banned. Too much of a dick. Not worth it.
11. ~~Sister Michael~~
    ~~(For proving she was wrong about me reasons)~~
    Banned. Is on power trip.
12. ~~Adittion: Michelle's Cousin John James~~
    Banned. Too English.

30TH MAY

We got our book reports back today. Sister Patrick may well disagree with me, but I stand by my opinion. 'Great Expectations' could do with a rewrite. It's quite sloppy in places. I much prefer 'The Catcher in the Rye'. Then again, I'm biased because Salinger and I have quite a similar style. Though obviously my work has a more contemporary edge.

I still simply cannot believe that Orla was actually allowed to review my diary. Or that she gave it one star out of five. Or that she got a better mark than me! But I've decided not to make a big thing out of it. It must be tough for Sister Patrick to have to teach someone with my talent. So when she does things like give me a **TOTALLY UNFAIR GRADE,** I think she's doing it to keep me grounded. I'm so far ahead of the rest of my class that she doesn't want me becoming complacent. She needs to keep me interested.

BOOK REPORT

Name	Orla McCool
Class	12A
Title of Book	ERIN'S DIARY by Erin Quinn
Summary of Plot	Erin is sixteen and wishes she had a boyfriend and a life. Nothing else really happens.
Did you ultimately enjoy this book?	No. It's boring.
Stars out of Five?	One.

Boring?!!

OUR LADY IMMACULATE COLLEGE

ANNUAL

TALENT SHOW

Do **YOU** have a song, a dance or a special skill to show the whole school?

This is your big chance!

Only £1 to enter!
(One entry per person/group/band)
Proceeds to the School Library Fund

*****NO MAGIC TRICKS ALLOWED*****

20th June

4pm

The talent show is coming up, but I don't think I'm going to enter it this year. I've got other things to concentrate on, like being **THE EDITOR OF THE SCHOOL MAGAZINE!**

'The Habit' is an informative yet satirical commentary on convent school life. This is such a huge opportunity for me. I can't quite believe it, really. Louise Kerr was supposed to be doing it but she's really sick, so she had to bow out. It's soooooo brilliant!

I quickly realised nobody else would be confident or indeed capable enough to step up to the plate so I made the brave decision to put myself forward. The others didn't say much but I could see there was an overwhelming sense of relief in the room. If I hadn't stepped up, the magazine's entire future would have been in jeopardy. They didn't have to tell me how grateful they were, I could see it in their eyes. They know I'm doing this for them, for the school and for poor Louise.

I wonder will I have to give the editorship up to Louise when/if she gets better???

No matter. A worry for another day. On **THIS** day, I am the editor.

Erin Quinn, Editor

"The editor of Irish magazine 'The Habit', Erin Quinn had this to say about the latest events."

Right...well, the deadline's not far off now! Better get to work!

6.30pm

I hate this house! The noise! Granda and Daddy went to do the big shop and lost Mammy's docket for her birthday photographs and now they're all downstairs roaring at each other. Orla keeps torturing me to watch her step aerobics routines and nobody seems to appreciate the enormous amount of pressure and stress I'm under at the moment. I'm sure Anna Wintour doesn't have to put up with this shit.

Daddy,

When you're doing the big shop, grab me a couple of bottles of Sun Glow – no lighter than deep mahogany. Also a jumbo can of firm hold hairspray and an exfoliating scrub – a good heavy duty one – I like it to lift the skin clean off me.

Don't worry about my fags, I'll pick them up from Dennis, he just got a load of Spanish ones in and they're half the price.

Sarah xxxx

21st JUNE

8.15am

Mammy dyed my school shirt pink. Not the look I was going for on my first day as editor-in-chief, but Jim across the road let me borrow his briefcase, so it's not all bad.

I can't wait to get in there and motivate my team! This is going to be the most exciting issue of 'The Habit' ever published!

11am

They all quit! Absolute bitches! Aisling said everyone thinks I'm cold and ruthless. They're obviously terrified by my drive and intimidated by my vision. I'll show them! I'm gonna rebuild this magazine from the ground up.

Meet the New Team

Name: Erin Quinn – Editor-in-Chief
Age: 16
Favourite Colour: Emerald Green
Favourite Book: 'The Catcher in the Rye'
Favourite Song:
'I Can't Be with You' – The Cranberries
Favourite Movie:
'Three Colours Blue'/'Beetlejuice'
Favourite Food: Chips
Celebrity Crush:
David Duchovny/Zack from 'Saved by the Bell'
Piece of Advice You Live Your Life By:
If you can dream it, you can achieve it!

Name: Clare Devlin
Age: 16
Favourite Colour: Baby blue
Favourite Book: 'To Kill a Mockingbird'
Favourite Song: Anything by Whitney Houston
Favourite Movie:
'The Little Mermaid'/'Heavenly Creatures'
Favourite Food: A Cowboy supper
Celebrity Crush: Leonardo DiCaprio is such a good-looking boy and I'm really into good-looking boys.
Piece of Advice You Live Your Life By:
Be the change you want to see in the world.

Name: Orla McCool
Age: 15¾
Favourite Colour: Stripes
Favourite Book: 'The Witches'
Favourite Song: 'King of the Swingers'
Favourite Movie: 'Ace Ventura: When Nature Calls'
Favourite Food: Coco Pops
Celebrity Crush: Dogtanian from 'Dogtanian and the Three Muskehounds'
Piece of Advice You Live Your Life By:
Always be prepared!

Name: Michelle Mallon
Age: 16
Favourite Colour: Red
Favourite Book: 'Misery'
Favourite Song: 'Tribal Dance' – 2 Unlimited
Favourite Movie: 'The Exorcist'
Favourite Food: Chicken Ball Special*
Celebrity Crush: How long have you got? Robbie Williams, Snoop Doggy Dogg, Luke Perry, Ray D'Arcy off 'The Den'*...
Piece of Advice You Live Your Life By: Just do it!

Name: James Maguire
Age: 16
Favourite Colour: Dark blue
Favourite Book: 'Lord of the Flies'/'The Princess Bride'
Favourite song: 'Everything Changes' – Take That
Favourite Movie: 'The Godfather'/'Ghost'
Favourite Food: I'd settle for anything with a vegetable in it at this stage.
Celebrity Crush:
Claire Danes/Libby from 'Neighbours'
Piece of Advice You Live Your Life By:
Try to stay calm.

Latest News: pages 8-9

See page 5 for Horoscopes

2pm

Okay, we're just going to start with a quick brainstorming session to kick things off.

3pm

Brainstorming.

4pm

Brainstorming.

5pm

School was dismissed over an hour ago. Really need to start writing some of these ideas up. But first we need to think of some ideas.

6pm

Okay, things are really flowing now. We've got some pretty cool features lined up.

On the chalkboard: NEW ISS 1) ANIMAL S 2) SHOES OF

☆ Brainstorming Ideas Session

ANIMALS THAT SORT OF LOOK LIKE FAMOUS PEOPLE

Michelle Pfeiffer - Cat. Is this why she played Catwoman??
Danny DeVito - Koala Bear
Claudia Schiffer - Giraffe
Winona Ryder - Bird
Snoop Doggy Dog - Dog
(Oh my God, **THAT'S WHY** he is called that)

SHOES OF THE WORLD

India - Sandals because it's boiling?
Russia - Boots because it's Baltic?
America - Trainers. They like
to be comfortable?

Other ideas
HATS OF THE WORLD??

8pm

Okay, I've made a bold decision. One that not everybody agrees with – Clare feels so strongly about it, she's resigned. I've decided to publish a piece from the magazine's 'Searching for Myself' story competition as our main feature. The moment I read it, I knew we had to. It was so poignant and incisive. And more importantly...we don't have anything else. Photographs of animals that look a bit like famous people and sketches of different shoes from around the world just won't cut it. I understand that 'Suffocation: the secret life of a gay teenager' is controversial – obviously that's why the writer decided to remain anonymous – but she entered this competition because she wanted people to hear her story. And now they will.

Clare's nervous about the backlash – or more precisely how Sister Michael will react. She has no journalistic integrity at all. But I will not be silenced!

♡
life

22ND JUNE

Sister Michael is saying we can't publish the story. She wants us to drop it and lead with 'Shoes of the World' instead. This is censorship!

So now I'm sitting in my bedroom searching for myself. Who is Erin Quinn? A coward? Someone who bows down to authority even when she knows it's wrong? Or someone strong enough to stand up and be counted?

I'm publishing that story. So help me God!

PS Aunt Sarah has a new man and he seems really weird.

PPS Mammy got her birthday photos back finally. I don't know what all the fuss was about. They're wile* looking.

THE HABIT

A MONTHLY SCHOOL PUBLICATION

Vol no. 287   FRIDAY 7th   Student Woes Edition

THE SECRET
★ LIFE OF A ★
LESBIAN!

Plus Animal Lookalikes

> Closets are for clothes – not for people!

**EXCLUSIVE INSIDE STORY
– ONE GIRL'S STRUGGLE!**

**RAINBOW RAGE
– SUPPORT GAY RIGHTS!**

**PEOPLE WHO LOOK
LIKE THEIR PETS!**

Suffocation: The Secret Life Of A Gay Teenager

"The is the first time I've told anyone"

I'm not going to tell you my name. But you know me. I go to the same school. I sit in the same classrooms. Get the same bus home. I'm just like you except…well, I'm Gay.

I haven't been able to say it out loud yet so I thought writing it down would be the next best thing.

The is the first time I've told anyone, actually. My parents don't know, neither do my friends. The truth is I've only just admitted it to myself.

I hoped and prayed that one day I'd wake up and these feelings would just go away – that I'd be "normal". Until then I'd just keep it a secret. I'd pretend I was just like all the other girls at school. I'd play along, I'd laugh about boys I fancied. Nobody would ever need find out.

But these feelings aren't just going to magically disappear. I realise that now. And pretending to be someone I'm not is getting exhausting. I can't play this part any longer. It's becoming more and more difficult to say things that aren't true. I've never been a very good liar and now…well, it feels like my words are choking me.

I just want to be able to be myself.

But I'm so scared. I'm scared of what my friends will think. Of how my family will react. And there's nobody I can talk to about it. Nobody at all.

I suppose that's why I decided to write this message. I don't know if anyone else out there is feeling the same way but if you are, I just wanted to say that you're not alone.

We're going to be okay. I know it's frightening…but we're going to be okay.

And to everyone else, being a teenager is hard enough, don't add to someone else's struggle. Please try to be kind.

Anon.

23RD JUNE

7pm

I can't believe it! It's Clare. Clare is the lesbian.

I don't understand any of this. I didn't know what to say to her. I was upset. I mean, maybe I have no right to be, but I was. I'm supposed to be her best friend and she couldn't trust me with something like this. I don't think I handled the whole thing very well, to be honest. I just keep thinking about all the times me and Michelle were banging on about boys and Clare just sat there quietly, not joining in. She couldn't, could she? She's had to hide this massive part of herself because she was so scared of what people might think. I feel like shit now. I'm going to call her and say sorry.

8pm

Clare's Mammy said she doesn't want to talk to me.

24tH JUNe

3pm

Thank God for the stupid talent show!

I can't believe I'm going to say this, but I was really proud of Orla today. I admit I don't really get the step aerobics thing, but she's passionate about it. Why shouldn't she get up on stage and do her thing?! She looked so happy, she didn't even notice all the whispering and sniggering. How dare they laugh at her?! I couldn't bear it. And neither could Clare. We both stood up and headed for the stage! So did Michelle and James. We danced beside Orla like eejits*. We didn't care what anybody thought. We have each other and that's the only thing that matters.

4pm

I just saw the news...

24TH AUGUST

That summer was a remarkable one. It was the summer we dared to dream. For generations we'd known nothing but violence, nothing but hatred, but finally we were saying enough is enough. Finally we were saying let's give peace a chance.

That's right...

We're going on the "Friends Across the Barricade" Integration Weekend!!

I'm really looking forward to it. I think it's so important that we reach across the political divide. But also, I've always had a thing for Protestant lads. Forbidden fruit, I guess.

FRIENDS
ACROSS THE
BARRICADE

25th AUGUST

9am

The gang are on their way round, then we'll be off! Must remember to stop off at the shop and pick up a present for the Protestants.

11pm

Quite a lot to report!

1. On the surface, the Protestants seem normal enough.

2. We were wearing our rainbow pins because we have a gay friend. They do not have a gay friend. We are therefore more liberal. Win for the Catholics.

3. The Protestants do, however, have a friend who is deaf in one ear. Win for the Protestants.

4. One of the Protestants is a massive ride*. Like, seriously, he could be in a boy band. Good news.

5. Michelle has claimed the good-looking Protestant for herself. Bad news.

6. I intend to undermine Michelle and make the good-looking Prod fall in love with me.

7. I have not fully figured out how to achieve point six.

8. There appears to be a Protestant version of Sister Michael. Didn't catch her name but she looks terrifying.

9. Father Peter is here.

10. What was I thinking? He is an absolute dose*.

11. Though at least his hair's grown back.

12. Protestants don't seem to like Rolos.

We are going to go to the Protestants' dorm as soon as the coast is clear. Tonight is going to be epic!

Catholic gravy is all bisto

Fish on friday!

Protestants think Catholics are all alco's

DIFFERE

Holidays — Protestants keep toasters

Catholics go to Bundoran.

British vs. Iris

Protestants go to Newcastle

Richer

Protestants like

Catholics ♥ Mary

Cathlolics love s

Protestants love soup

Catholics like to

Catholics watch RTE

Protestants love

Protestants LOVE ACCORDIAN

Catholics obsesse

Bands + orange stuff

Catholics must ob

Distance between the eyes

Protestants Love

Holy water (Ca

Catholics love accord

Protestants L

Catholics ha

Protestants

ICES

PROTESTANTS SAY AN EXTRA BIT AT THE END OF OUR FATHER AND ALSO CALL IT 'THE LORD'? PRAYER

HOLY SHOPS!

Pilgramages

Sunday School

...olics LOVE J.F.K.

cupboards

...ck's day Vs. 12th July

...re freeries

...all

Mo

ues

...esto

...ve flutes

Biago

...ve horses +

...jilets

Vs football

...gie V hockey

Protestants think Catholics keep coal in the bath

26TH AUGUST

1am

Foiled by Jenny Joyce again! She reported us to Sister Michael just as things were really heating up. But before she killed the craic*, there were some interesting developments. Dee, one of the Protestant lads, was really chatting me up. Now he's not as hot as the hot one (who I think might be called Harry), but he's not bad. I was seriously considering him as an option when Michelle informed me that hot Harry (I mean, I'm pretty sure it's Harry) really buzzes off his virginity. Michelle had no time for that — she's quite keen to move to the next level whereas I'm more open to...well, taking what I can get. Michelle suggested we swap. Which I think might be a really good idea, actually. James and Orla were chatting to a fella called Jon, they all seemed to be getting on like a house on fire. And Clare was having a pretty intense discussion with Philip (deaf in one ear). We are totally nailing this integration craic*. Maybe we'll win a Peace Prize or something.

Erin,

I need some information. Can you find out in a subtle way if Michelle's mother was given the big bowl by someone she has since fallen out with, and if she can no longer bring herself to look at the big bowl because it's just too painful.

All the best,

Your mother, Mary

5pm

I can't believe we had to come home early! I blame Father Peter. None of this would have happened if it wasn't for abseiling.

Clare is still in shock. I suppose in a few short seconds she did go from a caring, politically engaged young woman to a sectarian lout shouting "Jaffa* Bastard" while dangling off a cliff face.

We all have to write letters to the Protestant school apologising for our conduct. I don't understand why the Protestants aren't being asked to apologise. Blatant discrimination. It's as though the Civil Rights Movement never happened.

Oh, Jenny Joyce got her brace off and, to be fair, her teeth do look cracker*.

Dear Protestants,

I hope this letter finds you well. I'm writing on behalf of me and my friends to offer our humble and most sincere apologies for what happened on our cross-community relations weekend, or "Friends Across the Barricade" as it is more commonly known.

Firstly, Michelle and I are extremely sorry for trying to swap two of you – and for implying all Protestants are the same. We appreciate you are all unique and have your own separate identities. By the way, I hope you don't mind the fact that I haven't written to each of you individually but I just couldn't remember your names. Secondly, James should never have used such sexist and derogatory language. Though it is worth noting, and this is in no way an excuse, that he is English and therefore has a much lower IQ than the rest of us.

Clare is mortified that she used the word "Jaffa*". She now fully appreciates how offensive it is – but she was also keen for me to point out that "Jaffa Cakes are lovely", so from her point of view it does hold some positive connotations.

We deeply regret upsetting you and hope you can find it in your hearts to forgive us.

Yours truly,

Erin Quinn

PS Orla maintains that she didn't threaten anyone with a knife and that you're all liars.

Mary,

I hear you've been asking questions about "The Big Bowl" and

why I didn't want it back. I mean, you could have just come to me

directly but I can understand you might not want to be seen looking

a gift horse in the mouth. Anyway, let me fill you in.

The thing is nobody does a dish in this bloody house, well, not

unless I nag the life out of them and I'm sick of it. So I've decided

to give every piece of crockery I own away, bit by bit. So far I've got

rid of all the side plates, three egg cups, the bread bin and of course

the big bowl. If they don't clean up after themselves, they can eat off

the fecking floor like the animals they are.

All the best,

Deidre

PS None of them have noticed yet.

31St AUGUSt

Oh my God! So it was Kerry Coyle's sixteenth last night. Kerry's this girl in our French class who sort of looks like a hamster but in a good way. Anyway, it was probably the best night of my life! John Paul O'Reilly kissed me! John Paul is seriously one of the biggest rides* in Derry. It was so romantic. I mean, it didn't last long because...well, he fell asleep. He has this part-time job in Burtons, which is pretty full on, so I think he was just absolutely shattered. I asked his friend for his number, but I think I must have written it down wrong because when I rang it, I got through to Radio Foyle. I could kick myself!

3RD SEPTEMBER

Second day of the new school year and I'm already sick of Jenny Joyce.
This whole "Vote for your Class President" crap is just so annoying. It's
not a real thing. Jenny's just created it because she's seen 'Clueless' and
wants to go to an American high school. Obviously, she's going to win it.
She's the only person running. It's all because she likes the idea of being
a president. She's an egomaniac.

I mean, I suppose it does sound pretty good.

"Class President Erin Quinn".

"A word from Class President Erin Quinn".

"Please welcome to the stage your Class President, Erin Quinn."

Maybe I should make this thing a little bit more interesting...

6TH SEPTEMBER

Jenny is furious! God, but she's so entitled. She doesn't think anybody
even has the right to challenge her. She must be quaking. I'm way more
popular than her. Me and the gang are gonna work on my campaign
tonight. There was a bit of bribery involved. I had to promise them all
a Chicken Ball Special*.

Let the games begin!

ERiN Quinn

FOR THE WIN!

JENNY JOYCE

WILL BE YOUR VOICE

7tH SePteMBeR

One thing became clear today. Jenny has serious resources. I walked
into school today only to be met with "Joyce for President" banners,
streamers, balloons — you name it. Aisling was handing out pencils with
Jenny's name on them. Actual pencils! I can't compete with that. A lot of
girls at our school have a stationery fetish so this is essentially buying
their vote. Talk about playing dirty. We're gonna have to get creative.

Manifesto

Aims:

- Write and direct a school play every month.

- Campaign to be allowed to wear trousers as part of uniform.

- PE should be optional.

- No more singing in assemblies.

- Start a poetry club – so like-minded people can create in a safe supportive space.

- Full-length mirrors in toilets.

- Be allowed to call teachers by their first name.

- More chairs in tuck shop area.

- Canteen to serve curry three days a week.

8th September

The big vote's tomorrow! Jenny might have been able to throw money at her campaign, but I'm a woman of the people. The other girls can relate to me. I'm likeable, I'm approachable...but most importantly, I care. I want to make this school a better environment for all of us. This isn't just some stupid popularity contest for me...I want to evoke real change. I've sent the gang out to do a quick opinion poll around the school...just to give us some sense of what way people are going to vote...I don't want to sound cocky, but I'm pretty confident that I'm going to be sitting on a landslide victory by tomorrow lunchtime.

Name: Caroline Leddy 12B

How will you be voting in the presidential election?

I'll be voting for Jenny Joyce.

Why?

I think she's got good experience because she's a prefect and I don't really think Erin Quinn is taking it seriously.

Name: Liz Lewin 11A

How will you be voting in the presidential election?

I'll be voting for Jenny for president.

Why?

She gave me a free pencil.

9tH SePtemBeR

8am

Okay, so looking at the polls, it seems there's a little bit of work to do. Perhaps one or two people still need convincing, but I'm not overly concerned. Jenny and I both have to give a speech in assembly this morning. I was up half the night writing mine and, honestly, I shocked myself. It's powerful stuff. There's no way it won't swing it for me.

12pm

Dear Jesus! I cried. I cried at my own speech. In front of the entire school. I just got a bit carried away because...well, it was just so moving and before I knew it, the tears were coming and it was too late to stop them and everyone was just staring at me – open-mouthed. All Jenny did was list a load of new social events she plans to introduce like the cold, emotionless robot that she is. I mean, crying at your own speech is a bit of an unusual move...but I think people will appreciate my passion.

My fellow pupils,

I'm not going to stand here and make fancy promises I can't keep. That's not what this is about. I want to offer you just one thing. Hope.

Growing up is never easy. Growing up amidst a bloody civil war harder still.

But you can still dream.

You can still reach for something better.

You can still achieve whatever you set your mind to.

I know that can be difficult to believe sometimes, but it's true.

I want to hear your ambitions. I want to help you realise them.

Let me.

Let me be your champion, your mentor, your friend.

Not so long ago, many Catholics in this city were deprived of their right to vote.

So please remember what our grandparents and our parents fought for.

Use your vote today.

Let me be your President.

Thank you.

3pm

So the votes are in and Jenny won. I demanded a recount, but Sister Michael said a majority of 96 per cent was fairly conclusive. Michelle thinks the crying episode was the final nail in my coffin — that nobody wants a mentally unhinged president. I won't apologise for my dreams — I thought I could lead Our Lady Immaculate to greatness, but it turned out all anybody wanted was more school discos.

TOOT TOOT!!!

All aboard Jenny's

70s Groove Train!

PRIZE FOR BEST COSTUME

Calling all disco divas!
Born to boogie?
Feeling groovy?
Then head on down to:

Funky Town!

1ST NOV
7.30PM

£1.50
ENTRANCE

12th September

We got them! We got Take That tickets! Their first ever Northern Irish concert! We're gonna see Robbie, Gary, Mark, Jason and Howard in the actual flesh!!! I could boke* with excitement. We saved up for months, then yesterday we queued up outside Golden Discs for eight hours straight in the freezing cold...Clare thinks she might have frostbite — but we got the tickets and that's all that matters! Michelle had a class* idea. We thought we could write to them and offer to show them around Belfast. I mean, we're not actually that familiar with Belfast ourselves. But they don't need to know that. We've only been once before. Sister Patrick took us to the Lyric Theatre to see a production of 'The Crucible'. It was obviously great to get a chance to see such a seminal work about the effects of mass hysteria and a political commentary on McCarthyism...and also the fella playing John Proctor was an absolute ride*.

```
         BLOCK    ROW    SEAT
  006     31      V      115
         ENTER BY: BLUE SIDE
    WATERMAN STREET ENTERPRISES
      AND MARTIN NIGEL-SMITH
            PRESENT
    TAKE THAT
         PLUS GUESTS
      SATURDAY 14 OCTOBER
  KING'S HALL, BELFAST NORTHERN IRELAND
         009 15689 22569 2
```

```
         ENTER BY: BLUE SIDE
    WATERMAN STREET ENTERPRISES
      AND MARTIN NIGEL-SMITH
            PRESENT
    TAKE THAT
         PLUS GUESTS
      SATURDAY 14 OCTOBER
  KING'S HALL, BELFAST NORTHERN IRELAND
         009 15689 34432 4
```

Dear Gary, Robbie, Mark, Jason and Howard,

We realise you must get a lot of these letters but we're not like the other fans. We feel like we have a very deep, very real connection to you all. And we know our personalities would really complement yours. We think we'd really "click". We can't begin to tell you how much your music means to us. We know all the lyrics to your songs and most of the dance routines.

We are really looking forward to your concert in the King's Hall, Belfast. We heard you've never been to Northern Ireland before so we'd be happy to show you around. Honestly, it's no bother at all. Just write back and let us know where to meet you after the concert.

Love

Erin, Orla, Clare, Michelle and James

PS Promise we're not weirdos.

18th September

4pm

We got a new English teacher!

Sister Patrick has left. We have been wondering for ages who would dare replace her. I loathed Sister Patrick. Maybe loathed is too strong a word, but the woman had no passion. She approached literature like a maths puzzle: so many exam marks for Shakespeare, for Eliot, for Friel, multiplied by however many hackneyed old quotes that she forced everyone to learn and regurgitate in essays.

But Ms De Brún...well, she's different. I've never met a teacher like her before. I've never met anyone like her before. She's all hair and eyeliner and motorbikes and attitude. Even her name: De Brún. It's just so exotic. I think it must be French. I'm going to find out what it means.

Okay, apparently her name is Irish for Brown.

Anyway, we had our first lesson with her today and it was just... incredible. I felt like someone had just switched a light on inside of me and illuminated a whole world of thoughts and feelings and beliefs that I didn't even know I possessed.

When she ripped up our poetry, I felt a jolt of electricity. It was so freeing! To start again...to be reborn...

Orla McCool

My Troubles by Erin Quinn
The bullets fired on the streets
As I lie in my bed
Are nothing to the bullets
Being fired in my head.

Boys - Michelle Mallon
I think Boys are really class
Especially the ones
Who have a nice ass.

An English Rose Among Thorns - Anon
They scratch and they tear and they try to hurt me.
But my beauty shines through for all to see.
They think I'm not strong.
They are wrong.
They are wrong.

English Class - Clare Devlin
Books are just so much fun.
They take us to another world
And let us escape this one.
That's why I like English best.
Where will we go today?
What is our quest?

Flowers - Jenny Joyce
Some Flowers are tall.
Some Flowers are small.
Some Flowers barely grow at all.
Flowers are just like you and me.
No two people are the same you see.

I had to babysit Anna while Mammy and Daddy went on a date. Boke*.
Anyway, the gang came round to work on our poetry. We all felt so
inspired by Ms De Brún today. We just really want to impress her.
But writing from the soul is harder than it sounds. The only thing we
really achieved was the decimation of the Christmas cupboard.
Which I knew wasn't going to go down well with Mammy, who was
already in a bad mood – from what I could make out she'd had a falling
out with some fella called Keyser Söze. I think he must work in the
cinema or something.

Feel free to add your theories below.

Mary x

Who is Keyser S?

Gabriel Byrne (who by the way is getting better looking!)

Fella with the limp?

Pete Postlethwaite (brilliant actor!)

That fella they met in the desert (was it the desert? It looked
boiling anyway) Don't mind* his name but he was also in The Mask?

Alec Baldwin's wee brother?

Jim across the road? (outsider)

Replacement list for the Christmas cupboard

* 5 boxes of Tunnocks Teacakes

* 3 boxes of Snowballs

* 2 Tayto multipacks

* 24-can box of Coke — the good stuff

* A tin of Roses

* A tin of Quality Street

* A box of chocolate money

* 4 litres of red lemonade

* A bag of fun size Mars bars/Bountys/Milky Ways

* A whack* of Free State* chocolate

20th September

4pm

Ms De Brún has, like, lifted us to a new level. Gone are all my old preconceptions and beliefs. When she lined us up on the sports pitch and told us to whack that camogie ball as if it were something we hated, something we despised, it released this raw, animalistic energy – we all went wild! She's unlocked something in us and now there's no going back.

Although, Orla has since thrown out every single pair of socks she owns, which can't be hygienic.

I'd like to know more about Ms De Brún, about her personal life, I mean. I just have this feeling that she has a very dramatic and passionate past, with maybe a few love stories and broken hearts in far-off places. She seems that kind of person – free-spirited, spontaneous, uninhibited.

And I just love how she treats us like adults. Tonight she's invited us to her place to have a few glasses of wine. This is how it should be. We shouldn't be afraid of our teachers – they should be our mentors, our confidantes, our friends. She's just so open and honest and truthful – I've decided that's how I'm going to live my life from now on.

Had to tell my ma we're going to Michelle's house to study. Hope she doesn't suspect anything. Luckily, she still seems pretty preoccupied with this Keyser Söze fella. She would not be onboard with the wine thing. Apart from the odd sip of the blood of Christ at Sunday Mass, I'm not allowed to drink alcohol. She still thinks I haven't broken my confirmation pledge. The confirmation pledge thing really pisses me off – I mean, locking a child into a contract with **GOD** that they'll probably break is a bit lousy. Non-Catholic teenagers can have the odd bottle of Hooch without spending the whole next week thinking, "I promised God I wouldn't do that – I signed an agreement...Can he sue?"
It's so ridiculous.

In other news, Sister Michael is way too attached to that Child of Prague statue. I walked past her office at break time and she was having a full on conversation with him. I mean, it was very one-sided, as conversations go. Obviously, he wasn't talking back. Though I wouldn't put it past him. He's like something out of a horror film. I don't understand what she sees in him, to be honest.

11.30pm

I'm feeling kind of dizzy and I'm not sure if it's the red wine, or maybe a bit of a sugar hangover from yesterday, or just the heady, heady feeling of the shackles being freed in my mind, but what an evening! We went to Ms De Brún's house. She's an artist at heart. She certainly lives like one. Her flat is a blank space, a place for her to think without the distraction of possessions. I realised all the meaningless crap we think we need is actually burying us alive, weighing us down, suffocating us. I need to rid myself of all these shallow objects so I can breathe again. So I can see clearly.

(If Orla thinks she's getting my Sylvanian Family collection, she can think again! I'm hiding it.)

Miss De Brún quoted George Bernard Shaw. One of my favourite Irish writers.

(Double-check that Shaw actually is Irish.)

And I read one of my own poems to her.

The Glass Doll
By Erin De Winter

Be careful, child,
of the doll made of glass,
for if you hold her too tightly
she will break
and you will bleed

(Oh, I've changed my writing name to Erin De Winter. It's just got more gravitas.)

I was really hesitant to read it at first as it's so personal and deep, but I'm glad I did. She was so impressed. I felt for a second like our souls could speak to one another, woman to woman, artist to artist. The unbreakable, unshakeable bond of poets.

It was such a wonderful evening. The fact that we ran into Jenny Joyce on the way home didn't even ruin it. Although Clare was absolutely steaming*.

21St SePtemBeR

11.30am

It is unbearable. Ms De Brún has been fired! I blame Clare. She insulted
Jenny's mother (nonsensical insults but insults all the same) and Jenny,
seeking vengeance, must have gone straight to Sister Michael and
told her we were at Ms De Brún's house last night. Sister Michael,
obviously deeming this "inappropriate", sacked her! This is the worst
thing she's ever done to us! And yes, I am including the time she made us
declog the Sports Hall toilets. Well, she won't get away with it. We're
taking a stand this time. For Miss De Brún, for freedom of expression,
for ourselves.

11.30pm

It was the perfect plan. Until it wasn't. Sister Michael took away the
one person who managed to make us think, to make us feel...so we were
going after the only thing she cares about. The Child of Prague himself.

We were going to give him back, of course, on the condition that she reinstate Ms De Brón. It was bold, it was fearless and on reflection it was probably quite poorly thought through.

Sister Michael was at Judo — so the kidnapping itself was fairly straightforward. We knew he wouldn't put up a fight. He's a statue.

Then for stage two. We needed to send her a ransom note outlining our demands and a photograph of the victim. We headed to the Art department to "borrow" the school camera from the storeroom. Unfortunately, Jenny Joyce was there working on her Tutankhamun project – which, by the way, is completely over the top – I think the Pyramids are to scale – she's basically turned that classroom into the Valley of the Kings.

Jenny starts sticking her nose in, saying if we want the camera we need to have a permission slip. Things got physical and we ended up tying her to a chair.

Back in the English room, we put the final stages of our plan into motion. Taking the photographs...writing the ransom note...we were so fired up. There was no going back. We were gonna see this thing through!

But then, well, religious statues are actually quite fragile. And Sister Michael came back from Judo earlier than expected...so the bottom line is now we're all suspended.

The worst thing is it was all for nothing. Ms De Brón wasn't fired. She walked. Walked for holiday pay, a good pension and a decent mortgage rate. I feel so betrayed.

And to rub salt in my already festering wound, she "claims" she doesn't even remember my poem. My glass doll poem. I don't believe it. Not for a second.

Maybe she is jealous of my talent? If so, it's probably best she went. An insecure, envious teacher could really damage this critical stage of my creative development.

Oh, but Mammy did find out who Keyser Söze was in the end. She's absolutely buzzing*.

Right, I think I'm gonna hit the sack here.

Shit!!! We forgot to untie Jenny!!!

4th October

I've been thinking a lot about peace lately. Will it ever happen? This horrific conflict has raged on for so long now it can be easy to lose hope. We seem to be caught in this senseless cycle of violence. But what did violence ever achieve? As Gandhi once said, "An eye for an eye makes the whole world eyeless." (Double-check this quote.)

What if there were no guns and no bombs? If we could tear down the walls that divide us? What if we could respect each other's differences and work together to build a better future for ourselves and for those who follow us? But more importantly than any of this, I read an interview with Mark Owen in 'Just 17' and he said the reason him and the lads decided to include a Northern Irish date in their tour was because things had "calmed down there a bit lately".

Can you imagine how many cracker* bands would come here if we stopped killing each other on a long-term basis?!!! I feel very passionate about this whole peace thing now. It's vital that each and every one of us plays our part. I think I'm gonna ring John Hume's office* and volunteer my services to the cause. Not this weekend, though. I've too much on.

We were hoping Gary or Robbie or Mark or Jason or Howard would have replied to our letter by now but no joy. I suppose they're all flat out rehearsing for the concert. **I CANNOT WAIT!!!!**

Me and the gang are gonna start working on our banners tonight. We're really going to have to think outside the box if we want to grab their attention. The King's Hall has a capacity of 7,000.

Correction: "An eye for an eye makes the whole world blind." Gandhi

Robbie, Gary, Mark,

Wanna

If the answer

14TH OCTOBER

8am

Oh my God, today's the day!!! Take That, here we come!!! I kept changing my mind about my outfit but I've gone for my stripy bodysuit, maroon 501s (spoofs*, obviously) and this wee cream crochet waistcoat Aunt Sarah gave me. I don't want to sound too dying about myself, but I think I'm looking really well. I've a touch of the Louise Nurdings about me. So, assuming our banner does its job and grabs the lads' attention (it better — it took three hours to make and we used a litre of PVA glue), well, they're probably going to want to hang out after the gig. But where? We don't really want to go back to their hotel. They'll be trailed by fans and most Take That fans aren't like us. The majority of them are pretty deluded. We'd rather not have to deal with all that. So then we thought — between us we could just about afford a single room in the Europa — well, if James throws in all the birthday money his ma sent him. We can bring Robbie and the boys back there. We'll just sneak them out the stage door straight after their final number. That way we can all have a bit of craic* away from the spotlight. I think Gary and Robbie in particular would really appreciate that. And I'm sure they'd enjoy a night in the Europa. That place has such an interesting history — it's the most bombed hotel in the world.

10am

Okay, so Mammy said no chance are we staying overnight in Belfast. Daddy's gonna drive us up, wait for us and then drive us back again. This is obviously quite tricky. If Take That want to hang out with us, we'll now have to bring them back to Derry and there's no way they'll all fit in the car. We could squeeze one in at a push. Which probably means deciding between Robbie and Gary. Michelle and James are actually going to come to blows over this.

Although Mark could maybe be a compromise? He's also that bit smaller than the others so we'd have more leg room.

Could we put one of them in the boot??

No, Daddy's never go gonna for that after the whole Provo* Emmett (not his real name) affair.

10.30am

I HATE POLAR BEARS!!

I mean, I hated them anyway but this one's a special kind of arsehole. If it **HAD** to escape from the zoo, couldn't it at least have waited until the concert was over? Our mothers are now refusing to let us go. Aunt Sarah didn't help matters. She watched this documentary about a gang of polar bears who sneaked into a wee Russian village and started harassing this shopkeeper and his family. She's Mammy convinced they're all criminal masterminds. Mammy actually said if it was a lion or a tiger on the loose, she might let us take our chances...but a polar bear...no way.

Of course, this all is playing right into Granda's hands. He's been against us going to see Take That since the off. He hates concerts. His old friend Colette Doherty went to see The Beatles, or "thon shower of slippery scouse shitehawks" as he calls them, and then tragically died. The fact that the gig in question occurred in 1966 and she had a heart attack in 1991 leads me to believe Paul McCartney and Co. had feck all to do with it, but will he listen??

Now Jim across the road is saying he can tout our tickets and get the money back! **OVER MY DEAD BODY, JIM!**

11am

We're not going to just take this lying down. We will go to that
concert. So help me God, we will! We've come up with a plan.
We're going to get the 212 to Belfast. Our Mammies will never know.
We have an airtight cover story. Michelle is going to say she's at
my house. I'm going to say I'm at Clare's. Clare's going to say she's at
Orla's. Orla's going to say she's at James's...who lives with Michelle...
hold on...who's James with??? Christ, this is actually quite confusing.
We may need to simplify it.

15th October

2am

I think this might possibly have been the best day of my life!

Though for a while it seemed like the stars were aligned against us.

Sister Michael hopping on the 212 Maiden City flyer was a particularly cruel twist of fate. I often wonder if Sister Michael had some kind of tracking device attached to us in first year. She didn't buy our Ulster Museum cover story. And once she started asking questions about Michelle's suitcase of vodka, it could have been all over. Luckily, the Brits* thought it might contain an incendiary device and blew it up before she got a chance to look inside. It's always quite exciting to see the wee bomb disposal robot. This one was really cute – he looked like Johnny 5 from 'Short Circuit'.

Basically, we'd now – through no fault of our own – caused a massive security alert on the Glenshane Pass. We toyed with coming clean but we decided that the best course of action would be to just leg it.

So it turns out Derry is further from Belfast than a map of Northern Ireland would have you believe. But we met some really interesting people along the way. A charming, chivalrous band of ~~gypsies~~ Travellers who heroically returned Clare's purse to her after she dropped it en route. We had a wonderful chat about our different cultures and I definitely wasn't accidentally offensive in any way.

Then there was Rita, who generously offered to give us a lift the rest of the way. A fascinating woman with a keen interest in opera and... drink driving...though perhaps the less said about that, the better. I mean, that sheep just came out of nowhere. It was its own stupid fault. The fact that Rita was under the influence is simply irrelevant. No jury in the land would convict her. At least I hope not...because we disposed of the body for her...which probably makes us accessories to murder.

Anyway, we made it!! We saw the fab five in the flesh!!! We managed to get really close to the stage as well, which did sort of involve getting into a physical fight with a couple of fans from Newry at one point and unfortunately Clare lost her favourite scrunchie. But it was so worth it. We were just metres from **THE ACTUAL TAKE THAT.** I honestly think I had an out of body experience at one point. Sadly, Michelle had put our banner in her suitcase and it was therefore blown to smithereens. **BUT** Jason blew me a kiss during 'Pray'!!!!! God, he's **SUCH** a flirt.

Rita's Top Five Classical Bangers

1. **Symphony No. 2 - Gustav Mahler**

   An epic evocation of life and death. Once the 'Resurrection' gets pumping, it's hard to beat.

2. **Cello Concerto in E Minor - Edward Elgar**

   Who would believe an Englishman could produce such an emotional rollercoaster. Fair play!

3. **Spem in Alium - Thomas Tallis**

   This absolutely fucking glorious Renaissance motet brings together a 40-voice harmony. Cracking stuff.

4. **Violin Concerto in D Major - Beethoven**

   The pinnacle of the repertoire for concert violinists. Once it gets going, it's better than riding.

5. **St Matthew Passion - J.S. Bach**

   The greatest piece of sacred music ever written. If you disagree, you're full of shite!

Dear Belfast Zoo,

I don't normally write letters of complaint because I. I have a life and B. I'm not a dick, but that polar bear of yours is an absolute arsehole.

He made me and my friends late for the Take That concert which meant I missed 'Sure', and my chance to feel Robbie Williams up because that was the ONLY time he did a walkabout. I am beyond fuming with the furry-faced fucker. He's one arrogant prick who thinks the rules don't apply to him and I can't understand why, he's nothing special – who even goes to the zoo to see polar bears?

I mean they're no lions. I actually feel really sorry for the people of Poland, having such ballbags as their national animal. Anyway East 17 are playing here next year so I hope you have your fucking house in order by then. I will not be amused if Dicko* goes sauntering* about Belfast again.

Michelle Mallon

Derry

. about
...ng on when my father
Francis took me to the Brandywell as
a six year old that day. More, pg 6

.... wearing the team

d
.es'
d to
ay da
A few
u watch
that UTV

.. not a myth,
30s really did
.ks, elasticated
..s and thick
. is also an almost
.efore the game
tly shuffle into
.. are very few
.olours and there
.ws what to do at

.et your first big
.ole generation of
.ptember 8th 1985
. the return of senior
. Derry, it was a first
to experience the
.ush of live sport at a

ESCAPED BEAR STALKS NI

A polar bear yesterday made an audacious escape from its confines within Belfast Zoo. The large mammal provoked panic amongst staff and local residents when it broke through the side of its enclosure, with the RUC advising locals to be alert for signs of polar bear presence. The creature proved itself to be quick on its feet, eluding keepers and animal behaviourists for several hours as it went walkabout around the countryside.

20th OctobeR

4.30pm

Orla's lurred* because they showed her drawing on 'The Den'* this

afternoon. It's a picture of Baby Anna's My Little Pony and it isn't even

that good. I've sent loads of poems in through the years, but Ray's never

bothered his hole* to read one out. I can't believe Orla still watches it,

to be honest. We're far too old now. She's such a wain*.

Dear The Den*,

You never read out any of my cousin's poems but

that's probably because they're boring.

So, here's a picture of my little pony.

Her name is Margaret. Isn't she cracker?

ORLA MCCOOL. AGE 16 ¹/₄. DERRY.

4.40pm

Oh my God, 'The Den'* are sending Orla out a goodie bag, and she's saying she's not sharing it with me! I'm telling Mammy!

4.45pm

I can't find Mammy anywhere. This is really weird!

NOTES

To whom it may concern:

Nobody in this house appreciates me and I'm fed up with lifting and laying the lot of you. You can all sort yourselves out from now on. I will be taking up residence in my room until further notice. Do not disturb me.

Regards

Mary Quinn

NOTES

To whom it may concern,

Me again.

Could someone please bring me up a cup of tea and a Wagon Wheel.

Leave them outside the door.

I don't wish to speak to anyone.

Regards

Mary Quinn

NOTES

To whom it may concern,

What happened in 'Coronation Street'?

Regards

Mary Quinn

25th October

Something so creepy happened to Clare tonight. Oh my God, I'm shaking just thinking about it. So she joined the school chess club. (I know. I know. I have tried to tell her this is not okay but she's panicking that she won't have enough extracurricular activities for her UCAS form.) Anyway, they were having their weekly meeting and afterwards Clare told the others to head on while she locked up. It was quite dark and as she was leaving, she saw a ghostly figure making its way down the corridor!! She let out a scream and the figure just disappeared into thin air! I always knew Our Lady Immaculate was haunted — the convent bit is, like, 150 years old. Who is this spirit stalking the school corridors? What happened them? What do they want? I simply have to find out!

26th October

Okay, so it turns out Clare didn't see a ghost last night. She saw Sister Michael in her judo gear.

31st October

Halloween night! We're all going as the Scooby gang! I'm a bit worried we're gonna be freezing at the fireworks — well, Orla will be okay because she's covered in fur, but James's dress is really short.

1st November

4.30pm

It's my cousin Caroline's wedding tomorrow. Technically, she's my second cousin. Or is she my first cousin once removed? She's Mammy's cousin's daughter. So she's Granny's brother's son's child, which means...

No, I can't work it out. It's melting my head.

Mammy said me and Orla can bring one friend to the reception... between us. Orla wants to take some girl called Tina Teaspoon, who I've not only never met but I'm not entirely convinced actually exists. Teaspoon isn't exactly a common surname in Derry.

4.45pm

Okay, I just called Michelle, and apparently Tina Teaspoon does exist. She works in the youth club tuck shop. Her actual name is Tina Bradley, but she once ate a whole roast dinner with a teaspoon, so the rest is history. There's no way we're bringing Tina Teaspoon to the reception. And I can't choose between the others so I'm just gonna ask all three of them.

Though, ultimately, I'm not sure they'll thank me for it — I think it's going to be a pretty dull day.

2ND NOVEMBER

Mammy killed my great-aunt Bridie!

We are the talk of the town.

Everybody is absolutely ripping* with her. Rightly so. You can't just go about hexing people. But I'm not going to challenge her! I'm not mad! I'm just gonna keep my head down and do what she says from now on.

To be fair to Mammy, the whole thing started because she was defending us. We'd had this fight with my cousin Eamonn — or is he my second cousin??

He's my great-aunt's son, which means he's Mammy's first cousin, which means...**MY GOD**, why does this have to be so complicated?

Anyway, the DJ started playing 'Rock the Boat' and Eamonn tried to join our line, but he is famous for getting the routine wrong. Like, it's not that hard to learn! We didn't want him cramping our style so we...let's just say we "encouraged" him to leave. Anyway, he goes crying to his Mammy, who then confronts my Mammy, which is when the "drop dead" comment occurred and, well...Bridie didn't need to be told twice.

I mean, things were bad enough before Mammy killed Bridie. Aunt Sarah hijacked the bridal procession wearing a full-length white dress — though, in her defence, she did look cracker*.

Oh and Michelle wants us to do drugs. We're all still debating it. I mean, drugs sort of don't appeal to me at all, but Shakespeare did do some of his best work while off his face on opium. Is it my duty as an artist to experiment? I can't decide.

We all have to go to Great-Aunt Bridie's wake later. I normally don't mind a good wake, but usually my mother hasn't killed the person in the coffin. This could be pretty awkward.

I've actually already planned my wake/funeral. I know that might sound a bit bleak to an ordinary normal person, but all artists are preoccupied with death to some degree. We're quite existential like that.

(Note to self: look up the meaning of existential.)

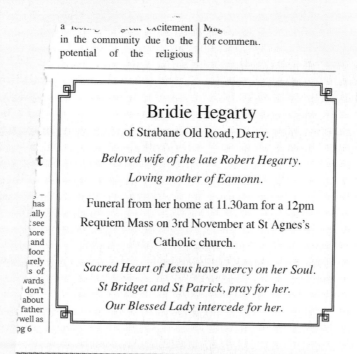

a ꞁꞁꞁꞁꞁꞁ ꞁꞁꞁꞁꞁ excitement Maぃ
in the community due to the | for commenぃ.
potential of the religious

t

has
ally
see
ore
and
loor
rely
s of
wards
don't
about
father
well as
pg 6

Bridie Hegarty
of Strabane Old Road, Derry.

Beloved wife of the late Robert Hegarty.
Loving mother of Eamonn.

Funeral from her home at 11.30am for a 12pm
Requiem Mass on 3rd November at St Agnes's
Catholic church.

Sacred Heart of Jesus have mercy on her Soul.
St Bridget and St Patrick, pray for her.
Our Blessed Lady intercede for her.

My Funeral Arrangements/Last Will and Testament

1. Glass coffin like Snow White.

2. Bury me in my blue satin slip dress.

3. Music – The Cranberries – sad anyway so will really tip people over the edge.

4. Readings – I'd like some of my poetry read out. Maybe Jenny Joyce could do it? I mean, I can't stand her but by God can she enunciate.

5. Do **NOT** use a picture of me with the fringe for my mass card/death notice.

6. Orla can have my Sylvanian Family collection.

7. My wee sister Anna can have the rights to my body of work and will be in charge of my estate.

8. Clare, Michelle and James can divide up the rest of my possessions as they see fit.

3RD NOVEMBER

It was Great-Aunt Bridie's funeral today. Eamonn's so pissed off with us. He kind of caught Mammy and Aunt Sarah trying to rob his mother's corpse at the wake — I mean, they had their reasons but on top of the whole 'hexing' fiasco, well, it didn't look great.

And then there was the unfortunate incident with his toilet and Michelle's hash scones and the clogging. I don't really want to go into it all but basically half of Derry now think I had a particularly aggressive bout of diarrhoea and my life is over.

I'm actually hiding upstairs in my room right now. Granda brought some of the hash scones home and every single member of my family got stuck in! Including Orla, who knew what was in them. They're all absolutely flying. Aunt Sarah is having a conversation with the pedal bin. I'm gonna stay up here until the manic laughter subsides.

It's not all bad, though. From now on, anytime Mammy says, "I've never taken an illegal drug in my life", I'm going to have a wee smirk to myself and she won't know why.

(Note to self: I looked up the meaning of existential — still none the wiser.)

9th November

8am

It is so exciting! The dance committee should be announcing the school formal today.

Me and the girls have been looking forward to this since we started at Our Lady Immaculate. What are we going to wear? Who are we going to bring? Everything has to be perfect. You only get one formal.

13th November

4pm

Right, we're not having a formal, it's going to be a prom. A fifties prom. What does that even mean??? Christ, but Jenny is such a dose*. If she thinks I'm gonna wear one of those stripy blazers her and Aisling had on in assembly, she can think again.

Our Lady Immaculate College

Invites you to partake in this year's

Fifties Prom

6pm 17th November

Don your best vintage frock

And get ready to rock!

We're gonna groove on down

To some old Motown!

It'll be Fabby Dabby Doo!

Get your tickets from Jenny or Aisling!

Oh, and a new girl started today. Her name is Mae Cheung and, wait for it...she's Chinese! I mean, she's Donegal Chinese, but it still counts. And she's agreed to be our friend!!! Jenny and Aisling tried to steal her, but they had nothing interesting to offer whereas we had a gay, so we won. We now officially have the most diverse friendship group in the school, with an English person, a lesbian **AND** a Chinese person. Jenny is absolutely Jack the Ripping*.

The switch from formal to prom started making more sense when we heard about "the vote".

Jenny's organising this whole thing just because she wants to be Derry's first ever Prom Queen – and by God, she is going to town! Christ, but that girl loves a title.

I mean, it's a bit pathetic, but I sort of don't care. Pulling together an event like this can't be easy – especially with Sister Michael breathing down your neck – so if Jenny wants to prance about in a cardboard crown, I say let her.

Erin,

Will you take this seriously! I really need to decide which of these fellas I'm gonna bring to the Prom. So Johnny Kells = Massive Ride*, but also very, very thick. Stupid fellas don't normally bother me, but he's actually simple. He saw a dead fish floating down the Foyle yesterday and told me it must have drowned. He's that thick, he's nearly clever, if you know what I mean? It melts my head. And then there's Decky R, who is definitely not as much of a ride*, but he's funny and he also knows how to show a girl a good time, if you get what I mean (sex wise!). It's so difficult. Maybe I should toss a coin?

Or just take them both, hahahaha.

Michelle

So Clare's quite worried about who to bring as a date because...well, there's a severe shortage of lesbians in Derry. So I'm going to offer to take her. And not just because I don't really have any other options...but because I always put friendship before fellas.

10pm

I am going to the prom with **JOHN PAUL O' REILLY!!!** This is the most significant thing to have happened to me in my entire life. I always knew we'd get back together.

I can't believe I'll actually be able to dance during a slow set for once. No more sitting on the wee chairs at the side pretending to be in deep in conversation with Clare.

Oh, speaking of Clare, I did ask her to be my date but then the whole John Paul thing came up and she totally understands. How could she not – even a lesbian must see he's a **MASSIVE, MASSIVE** ride*.

God, I'm so buzzing*! James said he isn't going to the prom. He wants to go to some robot convention thing instead. I feel a bit weird about it. It doesn't seem right somehow...him not being there. Although I'm sure I'll be too busy snogging the face off John Paul O'Ridey to miss him.

Worn with DMs as I'm a feminist

Monday Morning

By Jenny & The Jitterbugs

SINGALONG SHEET

Doobie doobie doobie doobie doobie doobie do x 2

It's Monday morning.

(Monday morning)

Hip hip hooray.

(Hip hip hooray)

Let's get going, it's a brand-new day.

It's Monday morning.

(Monday morning)

Come on let's go.

(Come on let's go)

Paint on a smile and start the show.

(Dum dum dum dum)

Oh Monday morning.

(Dum dum dum)

There ain't nothing

That I can't do.

(Doobie doobie do)

Oh Monday morning.

(Monday morning)

Oh Monday morning.

(Monday morning)

Oh Monday morning, I love you.

14th November

Clare was really off with me today. I don't think it's about the whole John Paul prom date thing. I mean, she knows we're meant to be together and I've promised her she'll be bridesmaid at our wedding — what more can I do?

I actually think this is about Mae. Clare is just so obsessed with her and so desperate for her approval. I'm also starting to wonder if Mae might be...I don't know...a bit of an arsehole?

I mean, I'm no Jenny Joyce fan, but Mae was pretty out of order about that dress in the shop. Jenny had left it over. That's all I was trying to say. But Mae just jumped down my throat and Clare took her side. I couldn't believe it! She's only known her for five minutes. Me and Clare have been best friends since primary two. I'm a bit upset about it all, to be honest.

15th November

I started a new play last night. Although it may contain some parallels with recent events in my life, it is in no way about Clare and her new annoying best friend Mae.

Emma stands at the sink in the school toilets washing her hands. Ciara enters. A moment of tension.

Emma: Hey.

Ciara: Look, I don't want an argument.

Emma: I'm just saying hello. Is that, like, illegal now?

Ciara: Whatever.

Emma: Why won't you even speak to me anymore? You walk past me in the corridor like we're strangers. We've been through so much together, ~~Clare~~ Ciara.

Ciara: Look I'm sorry it's come to this. But you shouldn't have said all those things about ~~Mae~~ Mona. She's new here. And you've been so awful.

Emma: I didn't say anything about her.

Ciara: That's not how Mona tells it.

Emma: I bet it isn't. Can't you see what she's doing, ~~Clare~~ Ciara? She's trying to break up our friendship. To punish me.

Ciara: Why would she want to punish you?

Emma: Because she's jealous of me of course.

Ciara: *(A moment of realisation)* That does make sense, actually.

16tH NovembeR

Still haven't spoken to Clare. Like I even care. Mae's welcome to her. I've got other things to think about. Like getting ready for a date with the biggest ride* in Derry!

I'm just going to write some guidelines for Mammy for what not to say when John Paul comes to pick me up.

1. You must not speak to John Paul apart from the obvious like "Hello", "How are you?" and "Goodbye".

2. But you can't just say nothing because I don't want him to think you're weird.

3. You are definitely not allowed to point out any childhood photos of me.

4. Please don't wear one of your jazzy jumpers.

5. Keep Granda away from John Paul at all times in case he interrogates/kills him.

6. You're not allowed to offer him any kind of refreshment in case he accepts and we have to hang around and make conversation.

I'm sure she'll be fine with those.

17th November

He stood me up. Christ, it was just so mortifying.

I'd created this perfect version of tonight in my head. I thought it would be romantic, like a movie...

Actually, it was exactly like a movie towards the end of the evening, a horror movie.

James totally saved the day. I mean, I know my ma sort of called him and told him to, but still. He was really looking forward to that creep convention and he missed it...for me. I'm actually kind of glad John Paul stood me up. I had such a good time with James. I just don't have to worry about impressing him, I can just relax and be myself. Because we're friends, I suppose. I also thought he looked really well in his tux... and his wee scarf. He's sort of handsome, I suppose...in his own way.

And I was right about Mae. She's unhinged. I mean, I can't stand Jenny but I've never planned to dump a bucket of tomato juice over her in front of the entire year. We tried to stop it, of course, but didn't quite make it so we all got absolutely clattered*.

Mammy was so buzzing* about the ceasefire, she didn't even care about the fact that my Easter dress was ruined. I'm just praying her good mood lasts. Good luck to Michelle explaining that credit card bill to her ma now that her frock can't be returned! I think I might light a candle for her, actually.

Sister Michael has asked us all to report to her office on Monday. I'm worried she thinks we were somehow in on "Tomato juice gate". Our Jenny-hating history would certainly give us motive. But I'm just going to go through the events of the evening in a calm, rational manner and I'm sure she'll realise I'm not only completely innocent of any wrongdoing, but I'm also pretty much the hero of the hour.

20th NOVEMBER

Detention.

21st NOVEMBER

Detention.

22ND NOVEMBER

Detention.

23RD NOVEMBER

Detention.

24th NOVEMBER

Detention.

UN... Journal

KODAK FILM 2 FOR 1 - FOR THIS AND
FURTHER OFFERS SEE IN STORE
60 THE ARCADE, MAIN STREET, DERRY

MORNING ED.   32 PAGES   ESTABLISHED 1772

IRA DECLARES
COMPLETE CEASEFIRE

The IRA has announced a ceasefire after its quarter of a century armed struggle with the British. Their statement said there would be a "complete cessation of all military operations". They are now willing to enter into inclusive talks about the political future of The North of Ireland.

25TH NOVEMBER

CHELSEA CLINTON
IS COMING TO DERRY!!!!!!!

EVERYBODY, REMAIN CALM!!!!!!

I think she's also bringing her ma and da.

26TH NOVEMBER

So, as far as I can make out, everybody's absolutely buzzing* about this ceasefire, especially John Hume* — who just cannot get enough of peace. And now that we've all stopped killing each other, he wants to keep it that way, so he invited Chelsea's da to Derry to help him work out a long-term plan.

Chelsea is therefore gonna be at a bit of a loose end. She could hang out with her ma, I suppose, but that's not gonna be much craic*. I mean, no offence to Hillary, she seems like a nice enough woman, but Chelsea will probably want to let her hair down with some people her own age. That's where we come in. We're gonna take her under our wing, show her the sights, make her feel welcome. All we want is for Chelsea to enjoy her visit to Derry. We have no other agenda.

Although, if she did want to invite us to the White House to say thank you, we probably wouldn't say no.

Dear Chelsea,

Our names are Erin, Orla, Clare, Michelle and James and we
live in Derry, Northern Ireland. We understand you will soon
be travelling here with your ma and da and if they're anything
like our parents... well, you'll be bored out of your tree. We
thought you might like to hang out with us. We could take you
swimming in Lisnagelvin Leisure Centre. It has this really class
wave machine and afterwards there's a wide range of drinks and
snacks available in the cafe. We were also thinking it must be
pretty difficult for a girl like yourself to meet boys. Being the
President's daughter would intimidate a lot of fellas, we imagine
- so if you want to practise any moves on James, feel free.
He's all yours. In the evening we could go to the Strand cinema
and watch a movie - you can choose.

   Anyway, let us know and have a safe flight.

   Erin, Orla, Clare, Michelle & James

   PS We think your hair is absolutely cracker*.

27th November

4.15pm

Oh my God! Lots of preparations being made for Chelsea Clinton's visit (with her ma and da). The secret service are everywhere! There's one on the roof of the house opposite right now! This is crazy!

4.30pm

Actually, scratch that. It wasn't a secret service agent. It was Jim across the road fixing his satellite dish.

29th November

8.15am

Still no word from Chelsea. I don't think our letter reached her in time. They're absolutely useless down in that sorting office.

Anyway, she's just landed in Belfast. They didn't fly Aer Lingus like I thought they would. They used some American airline – Air Force One, I think it's called?? Her da's turning on the Christmas lights at Belfast City Hall, then tomorrow I guess they'll all jump on an Ulsterbus and head straight here. Me and the girls think the best thing to do is just wait at the depot for them.

9pm

As if we're going to school tomorrow! I don't care if Sister Michael actually expels me, I am not missing Chelsea Clinton, and the others feel exactly the same way.

Hopefully, she won't expel me.

Oh, and something absolutely **MAD** happened this afternoon. So, we were in the shop having a lively discussion with Dennis concerning the number of states in America, when a car pulls up outside and this woman with nice eyebrows and quite a weird accent sticks her head out the window and tells us to get in. Obviously, my first thought was "Child Catcher", but it soon became clear that this was the infamous Cathy Maguire. James's mum!

James doesn't talk about her much so she's a bit of a mystery, but Mammy and Aunt Sarah went to school with her and I've been trying to gather as much information as I can. This is what they told me so far.

1. She always thought she was too good for this place. (Mammy)

2. She's had a lot of boyfriends. (Mammy)

3. Her hair is naturally quite frizzy. (Aunt Sarah)

4. She always puts herself first. (Mammy)

5. The eyebrows are hereditary. (Aunt Sarah)

James was pleased to see her, at least. In fact, I've never seen him so happy. He was beaming, which made me feel a bit sad for him. I mean, she just left him here and Michelle says she rarely calls or writes. She sounds pretty awful, to be honest...

I might go down and ask Mammy if she wants a cup of tea.

30th November

I'll never forget today. I know that. Not for as long as I live. The whole of Derry was at a standstill, the streets were packed with people, the city walls were draped with stars and stripes and the chanting grew louder and louder: "We want Bill! We want Bill!" It was overwhelming, all that hope. It really felt like something was finally changing. But I couldn't join in. I couldn't smile. You see, James told us he was leaving. That he was going to London with his mother. I was speechless. I didn't even manage to say goodbye.

Thank God he changed his mind. Whatever Michelle said to him worked.

But now I keep thinking, "What if he hadn't? What if he really had left?" And I just did nothing. Said nothing. There was so much I wanted to say. I suppose it doesn't even matter now. He's here. And he's staying here. This is where he belongs.

Dear James,

It feels a bit strange writing this. Even though I'll probably never actually show it to you. But it felt important that...
I don't know...that I had it on record or something. The fact is I can't imagine this place without you. I don't want to imagine it. We're better for having you here...at least I know I am. You're one of my best friends in the whole world, and if you were ever to leave, I'd miss you. I'd really miss you. So please...don't try anything like that again.

Erin xxx

BEST FRIEND

~ THE WHITE HOUSE ~

Office of the Press Secretary

(Belfast, Northern Ireland)

For Immediate Release November 30, 1995

REMARKS BY THE PRESIDENT

TO THE CITIZENS OF LONDONDERRY

Guild Hall Square, Derry,

Northern Ireland 3:20 P.M. (L)

. . . .

I ask you to build on the opportunity you have before you; to believe that the future can be better than the past; to work together because you have so much more to gain by working together than by drifting apart. Have the patience to work for a just and lasting peace. Reach for it. The United States will reach with you.

The further shore of that peace is within your reach.

Thank you, and God bless you all. (Applause.)

. . . .

END 3.30 P.M. (L)[1]

[1]'Proud traditions coming together', CNN Transcripts, www.edition.cnn.com/WORLD/9511/clinton_ireland/transcript.html [accessed 07 July 2020]